M000196593

ENSENADA & NORTHERN BAJA

NIKKI GOTH ITOI

Contents

ENSENADA & NORTHERN BAJA

TIJUANA, ROSARITO, AND TECATE

Whether you end up loving it or hating it, northwestern Baja makes a vivid first impression. As a dynamic border zone between Mexico and the United States, the region encompassing Tijuana, Rosarito, and Tecate has a complex, multicultural identity shaped by rapid economic growth, immigration, and the harsh reality of sharing a border with a much wealthier country. The change in scenery as you cross from Alta to Baja California is shocking and depressing. The lush green lawns and newly paved streets of San Diego become dusty roads and shantytowns on the outskirts of Tijuana, with signs of industrial pollution all around. Downtown Tijuana has modern skyscrapers, glitzy shopping malls, and wealthy residential neighborhoods, but

you have to walk or drive through the less attractive parts of the city to get to them.

As the gateway to Baja California, Tijuana lures hundreds of thousands of visitors a day to cross the border and spend their dollars. They come to shop, eat, and party. Some go home that day, others stay the weekend, and a few simply pass through on their way to coastal attractions farther south. Caesar salad, Tecate beer, Nortec music, and trendsetting nightclubs all are part of the experience.

Fewer than 80 kilometers east of the metropolis of Tijuana, laid-back Tecate is the oldest border town in Baja and maintains the feel of an authentic Mexican community.

South along the coast, beachside Rosarito is a favored weekend getaway for San Diego and

TIJUANA

HIGHLIGHTS

(**Zona Río:** The trendsetting clubs in Tijuana's upscale Zona Río pack thousands of people onto their dance floors every night (page 12).

(**Rosarito Beach:** A string of mega-clubs along Rosarito Beach provide 24/7 entertainment for college students from the United States during the annual spring break holiday (page 23).

(**Baja Studios:** The Hollywood theme park Xploration allows visitors to go behind the scenes of a working movie house to learn how to produce a blockbuster film (page 27).

(**Parque Hidalgo:** Food and festivities center around Tecate's shady plaza, making it a suitable launch point for a northern Baja adventure (page 31).

(**Tecate Brewery:** While in Tecate, tour the plant that produces Baja's most popular brew. Located on the site of the original keg brewery, today's operation uses modern, high-tech equipment to produce 40 million liters per month (page 32).

LOOK FOR (TO FIND RECOMMENDED SIGHTS, ACTIVITIES, DINING, AND LODGING.

Los Angeles residents, except during March and April, when spring breakers from across the western United States come to town.

The news of gruesome murders, kidnappings, and military interventions in all three of these cities in 2008 and 2009 has deterred many would-be travelers from visiting the border. Day-trippers, partiers, eco-tourists, and seasonal snowbirds decided to go elsewhere for the winter 2008 and 2009 seasons. Faced with extremely low demand, many outfitters have had to cancel longstanding trips to the region. It's a cycle that's going to be difficult to reverse.

But for every traveler who has decided Northern Baja is too risky, there are others who are following through on their plans. And most

of them are getting through the border region trouble-free. The violence is real, and it's scary, but it's not the whole story.

PLANNING YOUR TIME

Many travelers prefer to limit time in the border region in order to maximize time at Southern Baja destinations; however, Tijuana, Rosarito, and Tecate each have their own appeal. You might spend a day, a weekend, or, in the case of Rosarito, a whole week enjoying the culture and adjusting to the change of pace.

A popular weekend itinerary involves crossing from San Diego into Tijuana, heading south to Rosarito and Ensenada, then northeast via Mexico 3 and the Ruta del Vino (Wine Route) to exit at Tecate.

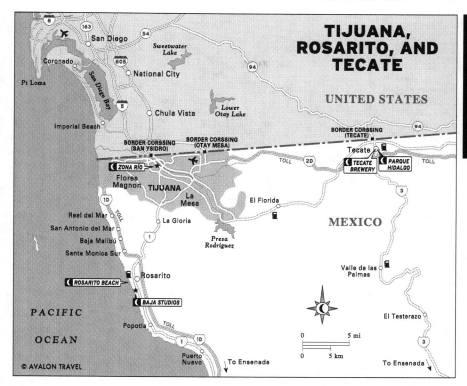

TIJUANA, ROSARITO, AND TECATE

If you're heading all the way to Baja California Sur, you can cover the length of Baja California (Norte) from Tijuana to Guerrero Negro in one long day, or, more comfortably, with a stopover in San Quintín or El Rosario.

Northwestern Baja enjoys a dry and comfortable climate year-round, much like Southern California. The beaches between Rosarito and Ensenada are warmest and most crowded July–September. Winter months tend to be cold and cloudy.

Tijuana and Vicinity

Straddling the Río Tijuana, now a canal, which empties into the Pacific Ocean, Tijuana encompasses a population of around 2.5 million (estimates range from 1.6 million to 3.5 million). Its urban sprawl covers deep canyons, hills, and plateaus in the northwest corner of Mexico. Most visitors come for the shopping, dining, and clubbing, but the city also draws people who want to drink underage, buy prescription medications over the counter, and visit its legal red-light district.

HISTORY

It may be hard to imagine today, but Tijuana wasn't always a border town. The Treaty of Hidalgo, signed in 1848, ceded Alta California

WHAT'S IN A NAME?

The origin of the name Tijuana is a matter of some dispute. In pre-Hispanic times, the Yumano tribes that lived here called the valley Ti-wan (Near the Sea), a name that the Spanish later changed to Tijuan on their early maps of the peninsula. A local ranch that dates back to the early 19th century called itself Rancho Tia Juana (Aunt Jane), which sounded similar but was easier to pronounce. Americans living in California adopted this pronunciation, and stuck to it, long after the city's name was officially decided as Tijuana.

to the United States and commenced Tijuana's rapid transformation from an insignificant cattle ranching settlement to a center of tourism, industry, and immigration. It was officially founded as Tijuana in 1889. Many U.S. citizens first heard of the city in 1911, one year after the Mexican Revolution, when a group of revolutionaries briefly occupied the town.

When the Panama-California fair took place in San Deigo in 1916, Tijuana put itself on the global tourism map, drawing a number of attendees over to the border for a concurrent Traditional Mexican Fair. With its lineup of arts and crafts, local foods, hot springs, horse racing, and boxing matches, the city made a lasting impression.

The U.S. Prohibition era brought foreigners over the border in greater numbers to drink and gamble. In 1928, the historic Agua Caliente hotel, casino, and spa opened to entertain elite Hollywood types, and the resort quickly became an icon of the growing city. The party lasted until 1935 when then-President Cárdenas outlawed gambling and closed Mexico's casinos, causing a severe recession.

By this point, however, the city was primed for growth through tourism and domestic immigration, and its population tripled from 1940 to 1950, from approximately 20,000 to more than 60,000, then exploded by 600 percent

between 1950 and 1970. An era of industrial development fueled the next wave of growth, with international companies opening hundreds of manufacturing plants called maquiladoras, which take advantage of cheaper labor costs to produce goods for export. Without the infrastructure to handle such explosive growth, Tijuana faced severe housing shortages and pollution. Collaboration between the United States and Mexico led to improvements through the end of the 20th century, and today, the standard of living is much improved—to the point where tens of thousands of U.S. nationals have made Tijuana their permanent residence.

Present-day Tijuana is a multicultural, cosmopolitan city facing a host of socio-economic challenges. Its dozens of universities draw students from all over the country. As the fourth-largest city in Mexico (after Mexico City, Guadalajara, and Monterrey), it also has the busiest international border crossing in the world, through which 40 million people pass each year. Tijuana has one of the highest income per capita of any city in the country, but as a border zone, it also must cope with a sizable immigrant population (legal and illegal, foreign and national), widespread poverty, and deep-rooted organized crime. In 2008, the city reported more than 800 murders, or 56.8 per 100,000 people, a rate that is lower than the comparable figure for several U.S. cities, but more than twice the number reported for 2007.

At its heart, multicultural, cosmopolitan Tijuana remains a young city searching to find its place in the world. Even as it struggles to cope with systemic crime and poverty, this urban community finds itself at the forefront of global trends in music and art. If it can find a way to harness and nurture that creative, edgy spirit, while at the same time restoring law and order, Tijuana could re-emerge as an economic and cultural leader in the region.

SIGHTS
◖ Zona Río

Officially called the Zona Urbana Río Tijuana, this part of the city borders the Tijuana River/Canal across from the *palacio municipal*. The

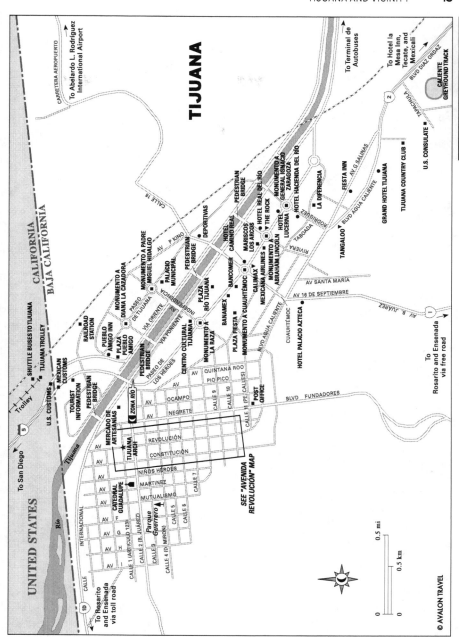

© AVALON TRAVEL

heart of the district is the **Plaza Río Tijuana** (Paseo de los Héroes btw Av. Independencia/ Blvd. Cuahutémoc), with dozens of shops and restaurants, several hotels, and some of the city's hottest dance clubs. In fact, the Zona Río boasts some of the largest and liveliest clubs in the world. A day trip here might encompass bargain shopping, a gourmet dinner and musical performance, and a night of drinking and dancing until the wee hours of the morning.

The Tijuana Cultural Center is a block away from the Plaza Réo Tijuana, across Avenida Independencia.

Centro Cultural Tijuana

Well-known Mexican architects Pedro Ramírez Vásquez and Manuel Rosen Morrison designed Tijuana's industrial-looking landmark, the Centro Cultural Tijuana (Paseo de los Héroes and Av. Independencia, tel. 664/684-1111, www.cecut.gob.mx), with a giant, white spherical planetarium (now an IMAX theater). The government-sponsored complex opened in 1982 with the goals of strengthening national identity in Northern Baja and promoting cultural tourism. Today, its 1,000-seat performing-arts theater hosts the Baja California Orchestra (OBC) and other performances (with some outdoor events in summer), and the **Museo de las Californias,** with historical, anthropological, and archaeological exhibits (Tues.–Fri. 10 A.M.–6:30 P.M., Sat.–Sun. 10 A.M.–4 P.M., US$2). The center also has a café, bookstore, and shops. Tickets are sold daily 10 A.M.–6 P.M.

Avenida Revolución

More shopping, dining, and nightlife are to be found along an eight-block stretch of Avenida Revolución (La Revo, in San Diego–speak), where the clubs are oriented toward a younger, Southern California crowd.

Tijuana Arch and Monumental Clock

This controversial addition to the skyline is located at Avenida Revolución and Primera, but it is visible from most of the city. To its backers,

AVENIDA REVOLUCIÓN

ZONA NORTE

TIJUANA ARCH ★
CANACO OFFICE ■
CALLE 1 ★
(ARTICULO 123)
TOURIST INFORMATION ■
TIJUANA WAX MUSEUM ★
CENTRAL DE AUTOBUSES
Pedestrian Walkway (Bars)
HOTEL NELSON ■
♥ HARD ROCK CAFÉ
BITAL ■
CALLE 2
(B. JUÁREZ)
■ BANAMEX
CALLE 3
(CARRILLO PUERTO)
IGUANAS RANAS ▼
SANBORNS CAFÉ ▼
CALLE 4
(D. MIRON)
BAR SAN MARCOS ▼
CAESAR'S SPORTS ▼ BAR & GRILL
HOTEL CAESAR ●
CALLE 5
(E. ZAPATA)
TILLY'S ▼ 5TH AVE
CALLE 6
(F. MAGON)
TERMINAL TURÍSTICA ■ TIJUANA
▼ MARGARITA VILLAGE
CALLE 7
(GALEANA)
▼ TIA JUANA TILLY'S
■ FRONTON JAI ALAI
HOTEL LA VILLA DE ZARAGOZA ●
CALLE 8
(HIDALGO)
■ POLICE STATION
▼ SANBORNS RESTAURANT/ DEPARTMENT STORE
■ FIRE STATION
■ BANCOMER
CALLE 9
(ZARAGOZA)
SCALE NOT AVAILABLE
▼ CALIMAX
CALLE 10
(SARABIA)
To Cava de Vinos and L.A. Cetto ▼
© AVALON TRAVEL

AV CONSTITUCIÓN
AV REVOLUCIÓN
AV MADERO

it's the symbolic gateway to Baja, but to most locals it's a visual hangover from the Y2K celebration. Either way, it's a good landmark to meet your friends after a long night in TJ.

SPORTS AND RECREATION
Golf
Founded in 1927 as part of the Agua Caliente Club complex, the **Club Campestre Tijuana,** or Tijuana Country Club (Blvd. Agua Caliente, tel. 664/681-7855, U.S. tel. 888/217-1165, www. tijuanacountryclub.com), off Boulevard Agua Caliente has a 6,800-yard, par-72, 18-hole course. The Mexican Open is played here on occasion. Greens fees are US$18–45. The club has a driving range and pro shop and offers golf lessons.

Baseball
Los Potros (The Colts, www.potrosdetijuana. com, US$10) play competitors in the Mexican-Pacific League as well as visiting teams from the United States and Central America. The 15,000-seat **Estadio de los Potros** (tel. 664/625-1056) is located off Boulevard Los Insurgentes near the Otay-Mesa border crossing. The season runs from the end of the American World Series through late January. Tickets often sell out, and parking is a challenge, so consider taking a cab.

ENTERTAINMENT AND EVENTS
There are myriad ways to spend an evening out in Tijuana, from professional sporting events and cultural performances to a night of drinking and clubbing.

Bullfighting
Traditional bullfights, though an increasingly controversial pastime, take place in the **Plaza de Toros Monumental** at the beach (La Playas de Tijuana, tel. 664/680-1808, www.plaza-monumental.com, US$10–50), off the toll road to Ensenada.

Dance Clubs
Most of Tijuana's top dance clubs enforce a dress code of no jeans or sneakers, and some insist on even more formal attire. The clubs begin to fill up around midnight and often stay open until dawn. The later the hour, the louder the music.

Trendy and formal, **Tangaloo** (Monterrey 3215, tel. 664/681-8091, www.tangaloo.com. mx), off Boulevard Agua Caliente, has taken over from Baby Rock as the hottest place to see and be seen. Dress accordingly, and pick a back-up option, as it may be impossible to get in. **Club Balak** (Plaza Pueblo Amigo, Vía Oriente, tel. 664/682-9222, plays Nortec DJ music, a fusion of classic *norteña* and techno music. **The Rock** (formerly Baby Rock, Av. Diego Rivera 1482, tel. 664/622-3800, daily until dawn) has been a favorite for many years for its laser-light shows and attentive staff.

A younger crowd frequents the clubs along Avenida Revolución—known locally as La Revo. Choices include **Club Animale** (Calle 3 and Av. Revolución), **Iguanas Ranas** (Calle 3 and Av. Revolución), **Tilly's** (Calle 7A and Av. Revolución, tel. 664/685-1612, weekends till 2 A.M.), and **Margarita Village** (Av. Revolución 702 and 1020, tel. 664/685-3862).

Mike's Disco (Av. Revolución 122, tel. 664/685-3534, nightly till 5 A.M.), on the east side of Revolución at Calle 6, is a gay and lesbian dance club with drag shows on weekends. On nearby Calle 7, **Los Equipales** (Calle 7/ Galeana 8236 at Av. Revolución, tel. 664/688-3006) is similar.

Bars
If dance music isn't your thing, Avenida Revolución has lots of bars—some historic, some divey, some fancy. Mariachi bands do their rounds, and the scene is usually a mix of locals, expats, and out-of-towners. **Bar San Marcos** (Calle 5 at Avenida Revolución, tel. 664/688-2794), adjoining Caesar's Sports Bar & Grill, has survived since its heyday in the 1950s. The Nortec Collective has composed a song about the **El Dandy Del Sur** (Calle 6 and Av. Revolución, tel. 664/688-0052), where the drinks keep flowing until dawn.

Large and loud, **La Cantina de los Remedios** (Av. Diego Riviera 2476, tel. 664/634-3087) in the Zona Río, is a chain with similar restaurant/bars in several cities on the mainland. Complimentary valet parking is a plus.

Tijuana's **Zona Norte,** from Calle 1 downtown north almost to the border, is the city's red-light district; it's best to avoid this area, especially at night.

SHOPPING

The majority of Tijuana visitors come to shop in the free trade zone (up to US$400). You'll find a long list of goods for sale, from arts and crafts souvenirs and hand-embroidered dresses to name-brand apparel and discount prescription drugs. You can pay with U.S. dollars anywhere in the city; some stores will also accept credit cards. Most of the stores along Avenida Revolución have someone who speaks English on staff.

Avenida Revolución between Calle 2 and Calle 9 has a concentration of upscale boutiques. For example, **Tolan** (Av. Revolución 1111 at Calle 7, tel. 664/688-3637) carries a nice selection of glassware, pottery, and other high-end arts and crafts. For a wider selection of pottery at lower prices than the boutiques, head to the **Mercado de Artesanías** (Av. Ocampo and Calle 2). Across from the Tijuana Cultural Center at Paseo de los Héroes and Avenida Independencia, **Mercado Hidalgo** is a more traditional farmers market with fresh produce and other foods.

Plaza Río Tijuana (Paseo de los Héroes btw Via Poniente/Blvd. Cuauhtémoc, www. plazariotijuana.com.mx) in the Zona Río, is a modern shopping mall with more than 100 businesses. The main department stores here include Comercial Mexicana, Dax, Solo Un Precio, and Dorian's. You can buy everything from a pair of glasses to jewelry and fine art.

A number of tile and furniture stores line Boulevard Agua Caliente between Avenida Revolución and the Caliente Greyhound Track. You can buy high-quality pieces made of wood or wrought iron at much lower prices than you'd pay in the United States or Canada. Just be sure to check the latest U.S. Customs regulations before filling up your car.

San Diego residents frequent **Sanborns** department store (Av. Revolución 1102 at Calle 8, tel. 664/688-1433, www.sanborns.com/mx) for English-language books, arts and crafts, medications, and liquor.

Tijuanenses buy their shoes, liquor, medications, and other day-to-day items on Avenida Constitución, one block west of Avenida Revolución. Prices are accordingly lower.

For last-minute souvenirs, or to pass the time at the border, browse the kitschy crafts in the indoor/outdoor **Plaza Viva Tijuana** (Av. Frontera and Av. de la Amistad), just before the border gate.

ACCOMMODATIONS

The hotel business in Tijuana is not well developed for a city of its size because the vast majority of visitors do not spend the night. The nicer places cater to business travelers from elsewhere in Mexico and overseas.

Under US$50

Safe and clean budget hotels are hard to find in downtown Tijuana. If you need to keep costs down, consider staying at the **Hostal Barnes** (Calle Relampago 1230, Seccion Dorado, no tel.), located outside of the downtown area at Playas Tijuana. It offers safe accommodations for US$10–15 per person. Private one- or two-bed rooms instead of dorm-style makes it a steal, but you'd have to bus or cab to La Revolución. If you can hold out for Ensenada, you can get nicer accommodations for a few bucks more.

In town, there are a couple of options for US$25 a night if all you need is a place to crash and shower after a night of partying on La Revo. **Hotel Lafayette** (Av. Revolución btw Calles 3/4, tel. 664/685-3940) is right in the center of the action, so you won't have to walk far to get home. But for the same price, **Catalina Hotel** (Calle 5 #2039 at Madero, tel. 664/685-9748) gets you off the main drag. Otherwise, it's a big jump up in cost to the lower-end business hotels.

US$50-100

Well-worn and centrally located **Hotel Nelson** (Av. Revolución 151, tel. 664/685-4302, fax

664/685-4304, US$50) has 92 clean, heated rooms with satellite TV and phones. Pack your earplugs. **Motel León** (Calle 7/Galeana 1937, west of Revolución, tel. 664/685-6320, US$90–110) offers 70 clean rooms with free, secure parking (though limited availability).

Hotel Palacio Azteca (Av. 16 de Septiembre/Blvd. Cuauhtémoc Sur 213, off Blvd. Agua Caliente, tel. 664/681-8100, toll-free U.S. tel. 888/901-372, www.hotelpalacio-azteca.com, US$80) provides above-average accommodations with large TVs, as well as heat and air-conditioning. Guests may use laundry facilities, as well as a swimming pool and parking lot.

Renovated in 2008, **Hotel Real del Río** (Calle J. M. Velazco 1409, tel. 664/634-3100, www.realdelrio.com, US$75) is a good value for business travelers, though street noise can be a nuisance.

C **Hotel Hacienda del Río** (Blvd. Sánchez Taboada 10606, tel. 664/684-8644, U.S. tel. 800/303-2684, www.bajainn.com, US$69) is reliable and modern business-oriented establishment with its own restaurant/bar, heated pool, fitness center, and business center. Choose from 130 large rooms and suites, which feature satellite TV, Internet access, and climate control. Ask for rooms at the back of the hotel facing the pool, since the front rooms are at ground level and face the road.

If you're driving and want to stay within walking distance of La Revolución, try the **Hotel La Villa de Zaragoza** (Av. Madero 1120 btw Calles 7/8, tel. 664/685-1832, www.hotellavilla.biz, US$60). Rooms are hit or miss, but your best bet is to ask for one of the garden rooms. Amenities include heat/air-conditioning, TVs, phones, parking, and laundry. Nonsmoking and accessible rooms are available. The security guards do a good job, but the front desk staff can be surly.

US$100-150

Your best choice in this price range is located in the Zona Río: **C** **Hotel Lucerna** (Av. Paseo de los Héroes 10902, tel. 664/633-3900, U.S./Canada tel. 800/582-3762, www.hotel-lucerna.

com.mx, US$120) has all of the amenities one would expect from a large, international business hotel: restaurants, pools, gardens, fitness center, and car rental desk. Ask for a room in the annex if one is available.

The **Grand Hotel Tijuana** (Blvd. Agua Caliente 4500, tel. 664/681-7000, U.S./Canada tel. 800/472-6385, www.grandhoteltij.com.mx, US$120) was one of Tijuana's first skyscrapers. With 22 floors and more than 400 rooms, it is a full-service resort, but the walls are thin and you can easily hear what your neighbor is watching on TV. The shopping area here has a ghost-town feel.

US$150-250

Business travelers and well-off weekenders like the **Hotel Camino Real** (Paseo de los Héroes 10305 and Cuauhtémoc, tel. 664/633-4000, U.S. tel. 800/722-6466, www.caminoreal.com, US$150) chain for its luxury amenities, such as marble baths and high-end toiletries; however, experiences at this property have been inconsistent in recent years. The rooms are underwhelming, but the staff generally makes up for it with top-tier service. Maria Bonita, its relatively new restaurant specializing in *alta cocina mexicana,* is open Monday–Saturday 1 P.M.–1 A.M. and Sunday 1–5 P.M.

FOOD

Aside from its shopping, bars, and nightlife, Tijuana is a culinary destination in its own right, with everything from cheap eats to haute cuisine.

Avenida Revolución and Vicinity

Caesar salad was invented in Tijuana by Italian-Mexican brothers Alex and Caesar Cardini in 1924. **C** **Caesar's Sports Bar & Grill** (Calle 5 at Avenida Revolución, tel. 664/685-1664, daily for lunch and dinner, mains US$10–15), located next to the Caesar Hotel, still carries on the tradition. A server prepares the salad at your table, and the key ingredient is coddled eggs, instead of raw.

The **Sanborns** department store chain has several of its popular *cafeterías* around town

(Av. Revolución at Calle 8, Av. Revolución btw Calles 3/4, Av. Revolución 737, and Plaza Río, tel. 664/668-1462, daily for breakfast, lunch, and dinner, mains US$10–15). The food is good, and so are the prices.

In business since 1947 under a couple different names, **Tia Juana Tilly's** (Calle 7 at Av. Revolución, tel. 664/685-6024, reservations tel. 664/685-1213, www.tiajuanatillys.com. mx, daily noon–midnight, Fri. and Sat. until 3 A.M., mains US$15 and up) is popular with locals and San Diego folks for Mexican dinners, as well as steaks and seafood. The friendly staff makes visitors feel welcome.

Zona Río

If you only have time for one "nice" dinner in Tijuana, call ◖ **La Diferencia** (Blvd. Sanchez Taboada 10611, Rio Tijuana, tel. 664/634-3346, www.ladiferencia.com.mx, Mon.–Thurs. noon–10:30 P.M., Fri.–Sat. noon–midnight, Sun. noon–8 P.M., US$10–23) for a reservation. The seasonally available Chile en Nogada or the duck with hibiscus flower (*jamaica*) sauce are standouts on an all-around excellent menu. Attentive service and a contemporary setting make the meal.

For truly authentic Mexican cuisine, **La Casa de Mole Poblano** (Blvd. Paseo de los Héroes 1501, tel. 664/634-6920, daily 10 A.M.–11 P.M., mains under US$10) matches its chili-chocolate, chili-almond, and sesame-seed sauces with a variety of meat and poultry. The high ceilings, ivy, and mariachi bands create an upbeat and family-friendly environment popular with locals.

A highlight on the menu at **Mariscos Los Arcos** (Blvd. Sánchez Taboada at Diego Rivera, tel. 664/686-4757, daily 8 A.M.–10 P.M., Thurs.–Sat. till midnight) is Mazatlán-style *pescado zarandeado*—a whole fish rubbed in herbs and spices, then seared and broiled.

Vips Restaurant Cafetería (Blvd. Sánchez Taboada 10750, tel. 664/634-6196, daily 7 A.M.–10 P.M., mains under US$10) is part of a large coffee-shop chain, and it offers a long list of breakfast and lunch fare, including Mexican plates. The locals like it, and it's affordable.

Agua Caliente

Check the specials menu on the blackboard on your way in at **La Querencia** (Escuadron 201 No. 3110 Sanchez Taboada at Blvd. Salinas, tel. 664/972-9940, www.laquerenciatj.com, mains US$10–25). It's easy to get distracted by the strange combination of safari decor and industrial chic. The lamb chops are well prepared and not oversauced. Just make sure your cab driver doesn't mistake it for the well-known La Diferencia.

Carnitas Uruapán (Blvd. Díaz Ordaz 550 opposite Plaza Patria, tel. 664/681-6181, daily 7 A.M.–5 A.M., mains US$10–15, cash only) sells housemade carnitas by the kilo for family-style dining. Sides include rice, beans, salsa, and guacamole.

Groceries

The two main grocery store chains in Tijuana are **Calimax** (Paseo de los Héroes, east of Blvd. Cuauhtémoc) and **Gigante** (Blvd. Aqua Caliente directly across from the greyhound racetrack or Juárez btw Calles 2/3). The Walmart-like **Ley** (Plaza Pueblo Amigo) has just about everything a traveler could need.

INFORMATION AND SERVICES
Tourist Assistance

The **Tourist Information Booth** (Av. Revolución at Calle 1, tel. 664/688-0555, Mon.–Fri. 8 A.M.–8 P.M., Sat.–Sun. 10 A.M.–3 P.M.) has a bilingual staff and the usual collection of maps and brochures covering Northern Baja. Additional booths are at the border crossing and the airport. The **Tijuana Convention and Visitors Bureau** (COTUCO, main office Paseo de los Héroes 9365-201, Zona Río, tel. 664/684-0537 or 664/684-0538, www.tijuanaonline.org. daily 9 A.M.–6 P.M.) has Visitor Information Centers set up at the pedestrian border crossing, the airport, and on Avenida Revolución between Calles 3/4. The privately run **Tijuana Tourism Board** (Blvd. Agua Caliente 4558-1108, tel. 664/686-1103, toll-free U.S./Canada tel. 888/775-2417, www.seetijuana.com) represents a group of local businesses.

The **Cámara Nacional de Comercio, Servicios y Turismo de Tijuana** (CANACO, Av. Revolución at Calle 1, tel. 664/684-0537, www.canacotijuana.com, Mon.–Fri. 9 A.M.–7 P.M.) has tourist information, mailing supplies, restrooms, and a public telephone.

For any questions that these organizations cannot answer, or for legal assistance, contact the **State Secretary of Tourism** (SECTUR, Plaza Patria, 3rd floor, Blvd. Díaz Ordaz, tel. 664/688-0555).

Money

You can use U.S. dollars just about everywhere in Tijuana, except for bus fare. The city has numerous ATMs, including a Banamex southeast of Plaza Fiesta and Plaza Zapato on Paseo de los Héroes. For currency exchange, a number of *casas de cambio* are set up along the pedestrian path from the border.

Post and Telephone

Tijuana's main post office (Calle 11 at Av. Negrete) is open Monday–Friday 8 A.M.–7 P.M.

Internet Access

Many hotels and coffee shops now have wireless Internet service for their patrons. Look along the northern end of Avenida Revolución if you need an Internet café.

Immigration and Customs

The Tijuana/San Ysidro border crossing processes all immigration and customs paperwork (daily 24/7)

Foreign Consulates

Visit the **U.S. Consulate** (Tapachula 96, Col. Hipódromo, tel. 664/622-7400, Mon.–Fri. 8 A.M.–5 P.M., closed U.S. and Mexican holidays) for help with lost or expired U.S. passports or visa issues. Other consulates in town include: **Canada** (Germán Gedovius 10411-101, Condominio del Parque, Zona Río, tel. 664/684-0461, Mon.–Fri. 9 A.M.–1 P.M.); **France** (Av. Revolución 1651, 3rd floor, tel. 664/681-3133, btdmex@telnor.net); **Germany**

TIJUANA PHONE NUMBERS

- Tijuana area code: 664
- Fire Department: 068
- General Hospital: 684-0922
- Green Angels: 624-3479
- Highway Patrol: 682-5285
- Immigration: 682-3439
- Police: 060
- Red Cross: 066
- State Police: 685-4444
- State Tourism Office: 688-0555
- Tourist Assistance: 078

(Cantera 400, Building 304, tel. 664/680-2512); and **United Kingdom** (Blvd. Salinas 1500, Col. Aviación, La Mesa, tel. 664/686-5320, fax 664/681-8402).

Green Angels

Mexico's Green Angels automotive emergency assistance service maintains headquarters at the Otay Mesa border crossing (Edificio Federal Garita, tel. 664/624-3479).

GETTING THERE
By Air

Tijuana has an international airport in Mesa de Otay, about 10 kilometers northeast of downtown: **Abelardo L. Rodríguez International Airport** (TIJ, tel. 664/607-8200, http://tijuana.aeropuertosgap.com.mx). Several international and discount airlines offer service to/from Tijuana, including:

- **Aeroméxico** (Plaza Río Tijuana 12-A1, Paseo de los Héroes, tel. 664/638-8444 or 800/021-4010, toll-free U.S. tel. 800/237-6639, www.aeromexico.com

- **Mexicana** (Edificio Fontana, Diego Rivera

UNITED STATES-MEXICO BORDER CROSSINGS

Crossing	Hours
Calexico (Mexicali) East	6 A.M.-midnight
Calexico (Mexicali) West	24 hrs/day
Los Algodones	6 A.M.-10 P.M.
Otay Mesa (Tijuana)	24 hrs/day
San Ysidro (Tijuana)	24 hrs/day
Tecate	5 A.M.-11 P.M.

Visit the U.S. Customs Border Protection website at http://apps.cbp.gov/bwt/index.asp to check border wait times before you cross.

1511 at Av. Paseo de los Héroes, tel. 664/634-6566, airport tel. 664/682-4184 or 800/509-8960, toll-free U.S./Canada tel. 800/531-7921)

- **Aero California** (Plaza Río Tijuana C-20, Paseo de los Héroes, tel. 664/684-2876, toll-free U.S. tel. 800/237-6225)

- Monterrey-based **Aviacsa** (Blvd. Sánchez Taboada 4499, Plaza Guadalupe 6, tel. 664/622-5024, airport tel. 664/683-8202 or 800/711-6733, toll-free U.S. tel. 888/528-4227, www.aviacsa.com)

- **Volaris** (www.volaris.com.mx) is one of a handful of low-cost carriers that fly in and out of Tijuana—an increasingly appealing way to mitigate the rising cost of airfare from LAX. It opened for business in 2006, and the best part about flying with this airline is that it runs a shuttle from the San Diego train station to the Tijuana airport (US$15), so travelers don't have to deal with driving themselves through the busy streets of Tijuana. From the shuttle pickup, it's a 30-minute drive to the airport, including a short stop at the border. The planes are new, and most of your fellow passengers will be gringos in the know. This is a great way to get to La Paz and Los Cabos in Baja California Sur.

- The airport has food, books, and gift shops, plus an ATM and parking garage.

- TIJ is an official port of entry for foreign pilots. Check with **Baja Bush Pilots** (www.bajabushpilots.com) for current information.

- **Airport Transportation:** Taxi service between the airport and any destination within the city limits costs US$12 for up to five passengers, and slightly less to the Central de Autobuses. Public buses signed "Centro" offer frequent connections to the downtown area (US$0.60 pp).

By Bus

Tijuana's **Central de Autobuses de Tijuana** is located five kilometers east of the city on Lázaro Cárdenas at Boulevard Arroyo Alamar (tel. 664/621-2982). It has a restaurant, *lonchería,* telephone service, immigration office, and currency exchange. **Transportes Norte de Sonora** (TNS) and **Autotransportes de Baja California** (ABC, tel. 664/621-2668, www.abc.com.mx) offer connections east to Mexicali

(US$9–12, nine buses/day) and the Mexican mainland. **Transportes de Pacífico** and **Chihuahuenses** offer more frequent connections to destinations on the mainland.

ABC's (tel. 664/621-2668, www.abc.com.mx) *ejecutivo* buses depart for Ensenada every half-hour 6 A.M.–midnight from the second Central de Autobuses (Av. Madero and Calle 1). Regular buses (no air-conditioning) leave for Ensenada from **Plaza Viva** at the border. ABC offers both *ejecutivo* and regular bus service to San Felipe as well.

Autotransportes Aguila offers intercity service to points south, including El Rosario, Santa Rosalía, and La Paz.

Greyhound (toll-free U.S. tel. 800/231-2222) buses from San Diego and Los Angeles arrive at the Tres Estrellas de Oro terminal (Av. México and Av. Madero, tel. 664/688-0082), which also has frequent ABC buses to Tecate.

Mexicoach out of San Ysidro has its own station at the Terminal Turística Tijuana (Av. Revolución btw Calles 6/7).

By Taxi

Taxi service from the border to downtown is about US$5 (flat rate); to Rosarito US$35 (one-way); to Ensenada US$100.

By Car

Most visitors heading to Tijuana by car cross at San Ysidro. You don't need a permit for your vehicle unless you plan to continue on to the mainland. You do need a validated tourist permit if you plan to go south of Maneadero or stay longer than 72 hours anywhere on the peninsula. A Mexican auto insurance policy is essential.

On Foot

A popular way to get to Tijuana from Southern California is to park at San Ysidro and walk across the border. The route is well marked and it takes about 15–20 minutes to get to Avenida Revolución this way. It you don't want to drive to the border, you can take the **Tijuana Trolley** (www.sdmts.com, daily 5 A.M.–12:40 A.M., US$2.50) from San Diego instead.

GETTING AROUND
By Bus

Tijuana has a complex bus system that can be useful for budget travelers or anyone who'd rather not have to negotiate with a taxi driver. As with other cities in Baja, the end destination of the bus is displayed in the windshield. You need pesos for the fare (around US$0.50). Walk along Avenida Constitución to find buses arriving and departing from the downtown area.

By Taxi

Taxi rides within the downtown area should cost less than US$5, and under US$15 to the airport or Central de Autobuses. You can pay in U.S. dollars. The yellow taxis that shuttle pedestrians from the border to downtown are a special breed. Drivers often ask more than the going rate of US$8, and they often get kickbacks from certain businesses downtown, so they may try to discourage you from going to the place you request. To avoid this hassle, consider taking a shuttle bus from the Tijuana Trolley terminal in San Ysidro to Avenida Revolución (US$1 pp).

Route taxis *(taxis de ruta)* are similar to buses, except the vehicles are station wagons that can hold up to 12 passengers and they stop wherever someone flags them down, which makes for more flexible transportation. Rates are slightly higher than the going bus fare.

By Car
RENTAL CARS

You can rent from any of several international chains, including Avis, Budget, Central, Dollar, Hertz, and National. Rates are lower here than in neighboring Ensenada or Mexicali. Reserve ahead, since fleets are small. When you arrive at the counter, you'll need to give a major credit card (not a debit card) as a deposit on the rental.

DRIVING

Traffic in Tijuana is heavy, though not insurmountable. Parking is another challenge. If you're used to navigating urban environments in the United States, you can probably figure it out here. Street parking is difficult along Avenida Revolución, but there are several pay lots open 24/7 for US$5 per day.

LEAVING TIJUANA
To the United States
To return to San Ysidro and Southern California, head north on Avenida Revolución and follow signs to San Diego. Avenida Padre Kino, north of the downtown area, is an alternative when traffic is heaviest. It connects you to the east lanes of the border crossing, which tend to be less crowded.

South to Rosarito and Ensenada
The 100-kilometer route from Tijuana to Ensenada is easy to follow. Most travelers these days take the four-lane toll road (*cuota*), Mexico 1-D, south, but you can also choose the two-lane *libre* (free road), which is the original Mexico 1. The toll road hugs the coast more closely, but offers fewer opportunities for stops.

To get on the toll road from downtown Tijuana, get on Calle 3 heading west and look for signs to Ensenada; traffic may crawl until the toll-road entrance near Playas de Tijuana. There are three tolls (*casetas de cobro*, US$2–3 each for regular passenger vehicles) along the way. You can pay in dollars or pesos, and your change may come in either currency depending on what the toll collector has on hand.

If you can manage to find it from downtown Tijuana, the *libre* follows an inland route at first and meets the coast at Rosarito. It then parallels the shore until La Misíon, when it heads into the mountains again. Access to the free road is not well marked downtown. Drive south along Avenida Revolución until it joins Boulevard Agua Caliente and watch for a sign that says A Rosarito (To Rosarito) and points right. Pass the Calimax store on the right and take the next right turn onto Boulevard Cuauhtémoc, which leads eventually to Mexico 1.

East to Tecate and Mexicali
If you want to travel east on the *libre*, take Boulevard Agua Caliente southeast. It will turn into Boulevard Díaz Ordaz and then Mexico 2. If you want to take the toll road to Tecate, follow the signs for the airport, not the signs for Tecate, which direct you toward the free road.

ISLAS LOS CORONADOS
A group of islands called Los Coronados lie within sight of shore 11 kilometers west of San Antonio de Mar, which is 12 kilometers south of Tijuana. The islands have a colorful past that includes pirates, rum-running, and a Prohibition-era casino known as the Coronado Islands Yacht Club. Steep terrain makes the islands impractical for habitation, but the Mexican navy maintains an outpost on one of them.

Geography and Natural History
The islands are the peaks of a submerged mountain range. The southernmost island is the largest at three kilometers long and 204 meters high. The northern island, Coronado del Norte, is one kilometer long and 142 meters high. The two islands in the middle are little more than rocky outcroppings. Since no one is allowed to land on the islands, they are popular nesting sites for brown pelicans and more 160 other species of birds. There is a large sea lion colony on the west side of Coronado del Norte.

Fishing and Diving
From April–October, yellowtail fishing is excellent around the islands. There are rock cod, bonito, calicos, and halibut.

Los Coronados offers good visibility for diving and playful sea lions. There aren't many large fish, but there are plentiful moray eels and schooling small fish. The main sites are the Lobster Shack, off the northeastern coast of Coronado del Norte, and the Keyhole archway at the south end of the same island. No regular dive boats frequent the islands, but San Diego–based **Horizon Charters** (U.S. tel. 858/277-7823, www.horizoncharters.com) will run a charter trip.

Rosarito and Vicinity

Once a quiet ranching community, Rosarito (pop. 73,000) has become something of a mini Las Vegas, only without the casinos. Development began in the 1920s with the opening of El Rosario Resort and Country Club, and reached a feverish pitch in the 1990s, when Fox Studios came to town. Rosarito's fate as a party town was sealed when the Hotel Festival Plaza built a huge entertainment complex right on the waterfront. The town's greatest appeal today—as then—is its long, sandy beach, which the high-rise hotels and luxury condos are slowly crowding out.

Until 1995, Rosarito belonged to the *municipio* (county) of Tijuana, and played a major role in funding the larger city's annual budget. Rosarito residents lobbied for 15 years to create their own *municipio,* so they could use the city's relatively high income to develop its own infrastructure and services rather than supporting Tijuana.

Tourism drives Rosarito's economy today, but like Tijuana and Tecate, the town has been severely affected by the wave of drug-related violence sweeping through northwestern Baja. To their credit, local authorities have taken steps to improve security, but many longtime Rosarito fans are staying away temporarily because it just doesn't seem worth the risk of being in the wrong place at the wrong time.

Many first-time visitors to Rosarito return home disappointed in the overall scene and their accommodations. This is a party town; on weekends and any day in the summer, the clubs rock until dawn. And chances are you will hear the music from your room, especially if you stay anywhere close to the main strip. March and April bring hoards of college kids on spring break, while an older crowd from Mexico and the United States visits during the peak summer months. If you know what you're in for, it can be a fun time, but if you're looking for a quiet escape in a boutique hotel, this definitely isn't the place.

Between Rosarito and Ensenada are a few beaches, coves, surf spots, and residential communities, collectively dubbed the Gold Coast by marketing-minded real estate developers.

SIGHTS
◖ Rosarito Beach

The action in Rosarito centers around the beach—an eight-kilometer-long stretch of sand. You can swim, snorkel, or surf here, but most people just come to relax on the beach and party at the clubs. North of the pier are several mega-clubs that provide beach chairs and drinks by day and DJ music at night. During the annual spring break holiday, college students from the United States invade the town and take full advantage of the 18-year-old drinking age. Horseback riding used to be another popular pastime, but it was banned in 2006. You can rent ATVs, fish from the pier, or just people-watch as you sunbathe.

Rosarito Beach Hotel

There are a few truly iconic hotels in Baja, and the Rosarito Beach Hotel (south end of Blvd. Juárez, tel. 661/612-1111, toll-free U.S. tel. 800/343-8582, www.rosaritobeachhotel.com) is one of them. It started as the only place to stay in Rosarito in the 1920s. During the 1940s and '50s, it became popular with the Hollywood crowd, counting Mickey Rooney, Lana Turner, and Orson Welles among its regulars.

The founder's nephew, a recent mayor of the town, became the new owner of the hotel in 1974. It has grown from 12 to 280 rooms, and its dramatic ocean pier anchors the Rosarito beach vista. The 500-meter pier (daily 10 A.M.–6 P.M.) is popular for sportfishing, but the height makes landing fish from the surface far below a challenge and the activity can be sporadic. Admission to the pier is US$1 for adults, free for children under 12. Fishing from the pier costs US$5 for the public.

TIJUANA

© PAUL ITOI

Rosarito Beach Hotel

SPORTS AND RECREATION
Surfing
There are at least 25 named surf breaks between Rosarito and Ensenada, far too many to cover in detail here. Some are over-hyped and packed with boards; others are consistent yet never crowded. Whether you are a beginner or an advanced surfer, you can probably find a spot that works for your skill level. For info break by break, pick up a copy of *The Surfer's Guide to Baja.*

ENTERTAINMENT AND EVENTS
Bars and Nightclubs
The best-known mega-club in town is **Papas and Beer** (Eucalipto 400 at Coronado, tel. 661/612/0444, www.papasandbeer.com), a huge entertainment center and nightclub covering about 4,600 square meters of sand with multiple bars, dance areas, and beach volleyball; the low cover charge keeps it packed on warm summer nights, but it's empty in winter. Papas and Beer celebrated its 25th anniversary in 2008. It has satellite locations in Ensenada and La Paz.

The open-bar policy at **Iggy's,** next to the Rosarito Beach Hotel, for the price of the cover (negotiable), can seem like a deal, but the drinks are often watered down. You can overcome that problem by working with the same bartender and tipping well. The crowds seem to pass by Señor Frogs located on Juárez and head straight for the beachside clubs.

Rene's Sports Bar (Km 28, Mexico 1, tel. 661/612-1061), next to Paraíso Ortiz at the south end of town, has pool tables and TVs for watching the game.

Festivals and Events
Aside from spring break, the best-known event in Rosarito is the **Rosarito-Ensenada 50-Mile Bicycle Ride,** which takes places twice a year, in April and September, and attracts thousands of cyclists. For more information, contact **Bicycling West** in San Diego (U.S. tel. 619/424-6084, www.rosaritoensenada.com). Even if you can't beat the course record of 2 hours and 13 minutes, you'll still have a great time.

The **Festival del Vino y la Langosta** (Festival of Wine and Lobster) takes place

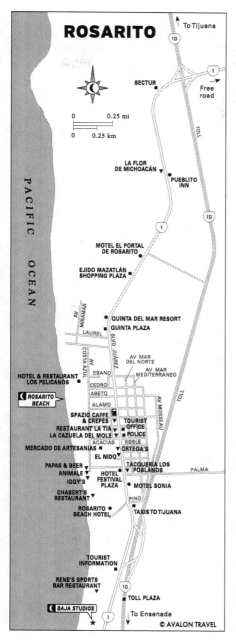

in October; call the local restaurant association, Cámara Nacional de la Industria Restaurantera (CANIRAC, tel. 661/612-0700), for information.

SHOPPING

Rosarito offers much of the same shopping you'll find in Tijuana, just on a smaller scale. There are handicrafts, furniture stores, leather shops, and art galleries.

For souvenirs, head to the **Mercado de Artesanías** (daily 9 A.M.–6 P.M.), on the west side of Boulevard Juárez, about midway between the Quinta del Mar and Rosarito Beach Hotel. This crafts market has hundreds of vendors selling all kinds of Mexican-made arts and crafts. Shop around and bargain to get a fair price for any items you buy. For beachwear and boutique shops, browse the many shopping plazas around town.

ACCOMMODATIONS

Most of Rosarito's hotels line busy Boulevard Juárez, which runs parallel to the beach. Condos and vacation homes are another option for travelers who want to cook some of their own meals. Contact the tourist office at the north end of town (Blvd. Juárez, tel./fax 661/612-0200, www.sectur.gob.mx, Mon.–Fri. 9 A.M.–7 P.M., weekends 10 A.M.–4 P.M.).

US$50-100

Originally built by the same family that established the Rosarito Beach Hotel and Rene's Sports Bar, **Motel Paraíso Ortiz** (Km. 28, Carr. Libre a Ensenada, tel. 661/612-1020, US$45–65) consists of simple beach cottages close to, but not on the beach, behind the Rosarito Beach Hotel. Comfortably removed from the noise of the main strip, **Hotel Los Pelicanos** (Ebano 113, tel. 661/612-0445, US$65) has 39 large rooms, all with heat and TV. On the north side of town, **Hotel Quinta Terranova** (Blvd. Juárez 25500, tel./fax 661/612-1650, www.hotelquintaterranova.iwarp.com, US$65–109) is pet friendly, as long as your pooch is well behaved and you bring proof of current vaccinations.

US$100-150

The **Rosarito Beach Hotel** (south end of Blvd. Juárez, tel. 661/612-1111, U.S. tel. 800/343-8582, www.rosaritobeachhotel.com, US$129) has evolved into an enormous complex over the years. Given the piecemeal construction of the hotel, the rooms can vary in age and decor. The newly opened Pacifico Tower has modern rooms. There have been enough complaints regarding the overall service and cleanliness that it merits a mention.

North of the Rosarito Beach Hotel, the **Hotel Festival Plaza** (Blvd. Juárez 1207, tel. 661/612-2950, U.S. tel. 888/295-9669, www.festivalplazahotel.com, US$100–160) is still the party epicenter in Rosarito for summer and spring break. Its proximity to the beach clubs keeps drawing the crowds, but in recent years readers have reported thefts and incidences of bedbugs and general disrepair at the hotel. The valet parking system is of particular concern, since you have to leave your keys with the staff. The hotel/entertainment complex includes a Ferris wheel and tequila bar, plus restaurants, clubs, and a heated swimming pool. The 114-room hotel section has basic rooms that have been frat-partied nearly to death. Suites, condos, and *casitas* are better, though pricier, options. Service tends to be a little better in the off-season. Wrist bands are required to enter the hotel, so you won't be able to invite that special someone back to your room unless they are staying at the hotel already.

FOOD

Most of Rosarito's many dining options are crowded along Boulevard Juárez. You can find everything from tacos to steak to seafood. Much of the food is adapted to gringo tastes. The larger hotels have their own restaurants as well.

C El Nido (Blvd. Juárez 67, tel. 661/612-1430, http://elnidorosarito.net, daily 8 A.M.–midnight, US$6–23), has great atmosphere and the food to back it up. The beef is grilled over an open fire. For breakfast, try the quail eggs and venison *machaca*. The restaurant's owner raises his own quail and red deer.

La Cazuela del Mole (Blvd. Juárez at Calle René Ortiz, tel. 661/612-2910, Wed.–Mon. noon–8 P.M., mains US$5), specializes in authentic sauces called *moles,* as well as house-made tamales.

La Flor de Michoacán (Blvd. Juárez 291, tel. 661/612-1858, daily 8 A.M.–10 P.M., mains US$5–10) still makes outstanding carnitas, and you can order them by the kilo (US$23–25 includes the usual sides of beans, guacamole, salsa, and tortillas).

Ortega's Place (Blvd. Juárez 200, tel. 661/612-0022, daily for breakfast, lunch, and dinner, mains US$15) is one of the original Puerto Nuevo lobster places, now with a restaurant in Rosarito. It still offers the lobster, but the buffet is more popular. Champagne brunch is a Sunday tradition.

Tacquería Los Poblanos (daily 11 A.M.–1 A.M.), on Boulevard Juárez across from the Festival Plaza, serves up spicy but good *tacos al pastor* for US$1. **Restaurant La Tía** (daily 8 A.M.–3:30 P.M.) sits across from the Pemex on the southwest side of Calle Ciprés, packed with locals and not a tourist in sight. It serves *birria*, chicken, or beef in chipotle sauce. Plates start at US$5.

For espresso drinks, **Cappuchino's Coffee and Pastry House,** is the place, diagonally across the street from Hotel Festival Plaza. Internet access is available. **Spazio Caffe & Crepes** (daily 8–10 P.M., US$4–6), across from the Banamex behind the Extra market on the southwest side of Juárez, is another option.

INFORMATION AND SERVICES
Tourist Assistance

The national **Secretaría de Turismo** (Secretary of Tourism or SECTUR, Calle Juan Ruiz de Alarcón 1572, Zona Río, tel. 664/682-3367, www.discoverbajacalifornia.com, Mon.–Fri. 9 A.M.–7 P.M., weekends 10 A.M.–4 P.M.) distributes information about local sights, accommodations, and restaurants.

Money

Rosarito has plenty of ATMs these days. For example, Banamex and Serfín have branches on Boulevard Juárez near the Hotel Festival Plaza.

GETTING THERE AND AROUND

Taxis de ruta make the 40-minute trip between Tijuana and Rosarito for about US$2 per person. You can hail one on Boulevard Juárez. These taxis can also provide service to the coastal towns south of Rosarito. The white-and-red taxis you see around town offer local service only.

Mexicoach (tel. 664/685-1470, U.S. tel. 619/428-9517, www.mexicoach.com) also runs shuttles between Tijuana and Rosarito (US$14 pp).

You can take the toll road (Mexico 1-D) or the free road (Mexico 1) from Tijuana to Rosarito. The distance is about the same, but the toll road is faster and easier to find.

If you're driving north out of Rosarito, follow the sign toward San Diego; the one for Tijuana puts you on the highway heading south to Ensenada.

Small shuttles called *calafias* are another way to get around locally on Boulevard Juárez. The fare is only a few pesos.

POPOTLA

Fifteen minutes south of Rosarito (6.5 km), around Km 33, a concrete arch in need of a paint job marks the entrance to Popotla, known for its collection of seafood vendors and other food stands. Menus are based on the catch of the day, which lands right there at the beach. It doesn't get much fresher than this, and prices are a little lower than what you'll pay in Rosarito or Puerto Nuevo. The stands begin serving around 11 A.M. daily. Turn off the *libre* just after you see the Xploration sign and studio.

◖ Baja Studios

In the 1990s, Twentieth Century Fox chose Popotla as the site for a massive US$25 million film studio, custom-designed for the production of its blockbuster, *Titanic*. Once the film was released, Fox decided to keep the studio and make it available to other filmmakers. Additional movies filmed here include *Master and Commander* (2003) and *Pearl Harbor*

(2001). Disney reportedly plans to film the next *Chronicles of Narnia* at Baja Studios.

A more recent addition to the complex, **Xploration** (Km 32.5, Mexico 1, tel. 661/612-4294, U.S. tel. 866/369-2252, www.xploration.com.mx, Wed.–Fri. 9 A.M.–5:30 P.M., Sat.–Sun. 10 A.M.–6:30 P.M., adult US$12, seniors and children 3–11 US$9, under three free), gives movie buffs an inside look at a working studio in a theme park–style experience.

The studio is about five kilometers south of Rosarito between Mexico 1-D and the beach. Exit the toll road at the exit for La Paloma, Popotla, and Calafia, and get on the *pibre* heading south. Look for the entrance at Km 32.8 on the *libre,* just before the arch that leads to the village of Popotla.

Accommodations

Near Popotla, **Las Rocas Resort and Spa** (Km 37.5, Mexico 1, tel. 661/614-0354, toll-free U.S./Canada tel. 888/527-7622, www.lasrocas.com, US$160) has a rustic feel with views of a popular surf break, fireplaces, and kitchenettes in its rooms. The rooms can be hit or miss, so ask to see one before you commit. Amenities include secured parking, cable TV, a restaurant, swimming pool, and hot tub. The hotel's on-site spa provides a full menu of treatments, such as massage and facials, and a steam room.

PUERTO NUEVO

Foodie alert: Baja's self-proclaimed lobster capital awaits in Puerto Nuevo at Km 44 at the north end of Bahía Descanso. Harvests have dwindled since the first in-home restaurants opened in the 1940s and '50s, and the scene is too touristy for some (mediocre food), but the village's lobster tradition is still going strong. Choose from dozens of seafood restaurants steps from the ocean (most listed at www.puertonuevolobster.com), which feature the signature lobster platter, with rice, beans, and tortillas on the side. There are a few different styles of presentation, including deep fried and grilled, *ranchera* style with tomatoes and chili, or just plain boiled.

Puerto Nuevo

If you happen to be traveling in mid-October, stop by for the **Festival del Vino y la Langosta** (Festival of Wine and Lobster, US$25 pp), which takes place in Puerto Nuevo's restaurant zone.

It's easy to find your way around the village, as it consists of only three blocks. Four streets run parallel to the ocean, and they are bound by the Avenida Rentaria (one-way toward the beach) to the north and Calle Barracuda (one-way toward the highway) to the south.

Misión El Descanso

Misión El Descanso (1817–1834) is one of the least-visited mission sites on the peninsula. It was founded by Dominican Padre Tomás de Ahumada in 1817, after the flood that washed away the crops at Misión San Miguel, just 13 kilometers to the south. The two missions were closely linked for the short time that El Descanso was in operation. A modern church is built on top of the original mission foundation.

Accommodations

The **Grand Baja Resort** (Km 44.5, Mexico 1, tel. 661/614-1493, U.S. tel. 877/315-1002, www.grandbaja.com, US$79–275), just south of Puerto Nuevo overlooks the Pacific Ocean. The views are great; the rest is not. Most units are in need of repairs, and the beds and linens are old. This is not the place for neat freaks.

A better bet is a rental home or condo in the **C Las Gaviotas** (one bedroom US$100–150) gated community, located eight miles south of Rosarito. Several property managers offer rentals in this development. Visit www.las-gaviotas or www.golasgaviotas.com for current listings.

Food

Prices are the same at most of the lobster houses, ranging US$15–30 for main dishes, and you'll need to pay in cash. Hours are generally 10 A.M.–8 P.M. weekdays, with later hours on Friday and Saturday nights. **Puerto Nuevo I** (S/N Av. Rentaria, no tel.) is the original Puerto Nuevo restaurant and still a perennial favorite. Next door, **Puerto Nuevo II** (Av. Rentaria 2, tel. 661/614-1454) is more upscale. These family-run places have been serving lobster for many years: **Chela's** (Arpon 15, tel. 661/614-1058), **La Escondida** (Anzuelo/

© PAUL ITOI

Paseo del Mar, no tel.), **El Galeón** (Anzuelo, no tel.) and **La Perlita** (Barracuda just west of the highway, tel. 661/614-1276).

LA FONDA AND LA MISIÓN

Mexico 1 *(libre)* and Mexico 1-D (toll road) diverge between La Fonda (a.k.a. K-58 or La Salina), on the coast at the southern end of Bahía Descanso, and La Misión, to the southeast (and not to be confused with Playa La Misión, which is a little south of La Fonda on Bahía Descanso). La Fonda offers the best beaches in the area, several of which have surfable waves. Take exit for La Misión–Alisitos from the toll road at Km 59.

Misión San Miguel Arcángel de la Frontera

East of the highway, historic Misión San Miguel Arcángel de la Frontera (1788–1833) is part of the Spanish mission trail in Baja. Dominican Padre Luis Salles came here from Misión Santo Tomás to the south, in search of a strategic point of connection between the Baja California missions and the newer Alta California missions that were under construction. Relatively little is known about the mission today, but it did grow corn and wheat and had around 400 indigenous people at its peak. A flood in 1816 destroyed much of the mission, and it was abandoned in 1833, at which point the population had declined to only 25. The scant remains of its adobe compound—just two walls in a present day schoolyard—are now protected by the Instituto Nacional de Antropología e Historia (INAH).

Accommodations and Food

La Fonda Hotel (Km. 59.5 Mex 1-D Rosarito–Ensenada Toll Road, tel. 646/155-0307, www. lafondamexico.com, US$85) is a quirky area classic. There are standard rooms as well as multi-room apartments with fireplaces and kitchenettes (US$100–150). Movement around the cliffside hotel involves numerous steep staircases, so if mobility is an issue, make sure to ask the front desk for an accessible room. The restaurant serves reliably tasty seafood and

steaks (mains US$12–25). Make sure to get a good seat on the terrace for the sunset, and if it gets chilly, the waiters bring small blankets and turn on the patio heaters.

Alisitos K-58 Surf Camp (Km. 58 Mex 1-D Rosarito–Ensenada Toll Road, tel. 646/155-0120, U.S. tel. 949/313-7059, www. alisitosk58.com, US$16) is a board shop and campground that can accommodate RVs. Amenities are few (flush toilets and cold showers), but the beach is a good one, and you can't complain about the price.

The **Poco Cielo Bed and Breakfast** (Km 59, tel. 646/155-0606, U.S. tel. 760/670-3336, www.pococielo.com, pococielo@yahoo.com) has four well-appointed rooms that are true to their themes down to the construction of the walls, murals, sinks, and sculpted entry rooms. A private stairwell leads down to the beach, and a new restaurant margaritas for US$7. It's a little Disneyland, but the good service and friendly owner make it a good choice for those looking to escape the bustle of Ensenada and Rosarito.

Baja Seasons (Km 72, tel. 646/155-4015, toll-free U.S. tel. 800/754-4190, www.bajaseasons.com) is a full-service resort with villas (US$140–250), motel rooms (US$80–120), and campsites suitable for tents or RVs (US$72 oceanfront or US$48 interior). You can only get to the park from the southbound toll road. Make a U-turn if you're driving north from the Ensenada area.

SAN MIGUEL AND EL SAUZAL

San Miguel and El Sauzal are neighboring communities on the Pacific coast, known primarily these days for good surf. In fact, San Miguel might be Baja's most consistent point break. It's located just south of the third toll booth on Mexico 1. Parking is US$5, and the crowds will be on it if the surf is good. Get there early to catch it before the onshores start up in the late morning.

Accommodations and Camping

◀ **Hostel Sauzal** (Av. L 344, tel. 646/174-6381, http://hostelsauzal.tripod.com, $15 pp) has been the starting point for many a Baja backpacking trip. It offers rare ocean-view hostel accommodations in dorm room bunks. Rates include bed linens, storage lockers, hot showers, continental breakfast, and bike/surfboard storage. Its four rooms have desks for writing letters and updating travel journals; plus there is a small library containing books, maps, and magazines. To find the hostel from the toll road southbound, go through the tollbooth at San Miguel and continue on the highway for about three more kilometers, passing under the footbridge. Next, turn left at a stoplight after the Pemex. Go two blocks and turn right; then one block more and turn left up a dirt road. The hostel is the third house on the right.

Several of the beaches along this stretch allow tent and RV camping for less than US$15 per night.

Tecate and Vicinity

Mountainous Tecate (pop. 120,000) sits at an elevation of 514 meters (1,690 ft) in the Sierra Juárez, which makes for a pleasant climate year-round. The highest peak nearby is the Mount Cuchimá, which straddles the U.S.–Mexico border. Protected by its geography from its industrial neighbors of Tijuana and Mexicali—and also from the extreme climates of the Pacific coast and San Felipe Desert—Tecate is an oasis of sorts along the international border zone. Fresh air and clean spring water led to the establishment of Tecate's two most famous enterprises: the Tecate Brewery and Rancho La Puerta health spa.

The town today is a quiet farming center, but it has also developed something an artistic side, with a small community of painters and writers in residence. Beyond the city limits, several rancho resorts and numerous aquatic recreation parks offer accommodations and entertainment.

Mexican-American writer Daniel Reveles

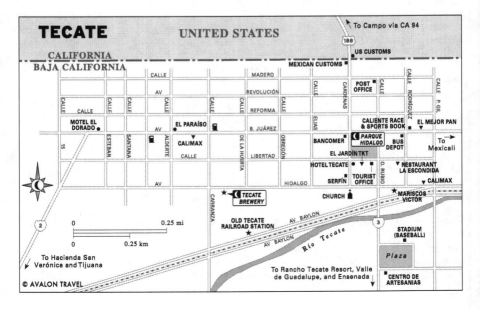

has written several books of short stories that take place in Tecate. They can be an enjoyable way to get acquainted with the town.

HISTORY

In its earliest history, the fertile valley and abundant water supply here supported a group of Yuma, who called the area Zacate (the most likely origin of the name Tecate). They believed the 1,520-meter Cerro Cuchumá (also spelled Kuchumaa) had important spiritual significance.

In the early 19th century, Mexicans began cultivating the land, and in the 1830s, a Peruvian named Juan Bandini founded the town with a land grant from the Mexican government. Later in the century, the government built a railroad to connect the three emerging border towns of Tijuana, Tecate, and Mexicali, and Tecate became the capital of its own Mexican municipality in 1892.

The most significant development in the city's history took place in 1943, when the Tecate Brewery opened for business. As the border zone industrialized later in the century, Tecate gained a number of maquiladoras, east of the city on Mexico 2. The economy today is mainly driven by farming, though tourism and manufacturing play smaller roles.

SIGHTS
◖ Parque Hidalgo

Tecate has five main parks within its limits, and the most popular is shady Parque Hidalgo (Av. Juárez and Calle Lázaro Cárdenas, Zona Centro). Built in 1952, this small park is the center of town life and gives the visitor a good sense of the place. A pretty gazebo and wrought-iron benches invite quiet contemplation. Eat ice cream and watch the locals play a game of dominoes. Note the statue of Miguel Hidalgo, the Dolores priest who issued the call for Mexican independence in 1810, in the southeast corner of the park. Surrounding the park are local government offices, restaurants, taco stands, and a few shops selling *artesanias*.

© JIMCLINE.COM

Tecate Brewery

◖ Tecate Brewery

Entreprenaur Alberto Aldrete came up with the idea for a brewery to complement his malt-making business. He ran out of money 10 years after creating Tecate beer, but a Monterrey businessman, Eugenio Garza Sada, bought the label and added it to the lineup offered by Cervecería Cuauhtémoc.

Canned Tecate is brewed in Monterrey, but bottles and kegs are made only in its namesake Tecate. If you've tried Tecate beer only in the United States, chances are you haven't experienced the real thing. Exported Tecate is made in Monterrey (not from the pure spring water of Tecate) and with a lower alcohol content than domestically consumed Tecate (3.2 percent compared to 3.6 percent).

The brewery today (Dr. Arturo Guerra 70, tel. 665/654-9478, www.ccm.com.mx, Mon.–Fri. 10 A.M.–noon and 3–4:30 P.M., Sat. 9–10:30 A.M.) occupies the same site as the original keg brewery; high-tech German equipment is used to produce 40 million liters per month and ship to 100 countries around the world.

Old Tecate Railroad Station

Built in 1915, the Old Tecate Railroad Station was part of a line that connected San Diego to Yuma, Arizona, and played an important role in the industrial development of the area. In its time, the station held a waiting room, office, and small warehouse on its ground floor, and a residence for the station master above. The station is now part of a small historic district, which includes the Tecate Brewery and is protected by the city.

The **Pacific Southwest Railway Museum** (State Hwy 94 and Forest Gate Rd., Campo, CA, U.S. weekend tel. 619/478-9937, U.S. weekday tel. 619/465-7776, www.sdrm.org, US$43) offers occasional Saturday rail trips from its Campo depot (80 minutes by car from downtown San Diego) to Tecate, 1.25-hour ride. Trains leave Campo at 10:30 A.M. and return at 4:30 P.M. In summer, twilight trips depart Campo at 3 P.M. and return at 9 P.M. Reservations are required. Credit cards and PayPal are accepted.

Walking Tour

A two-hour self-guided walking tour of Tecate begins on Avenida Juárez heading east from Parque Miguel Hidalgo. Cross Rubio and Rodríguez at Rodriguez and look for El Major Pan de Tecate Bakery on the next block. Retrace your steps to the park and cross through it to find the alley called Callejón Libertad and temporary art exhibits in the **Baja California Cultural Institute** (ICBC, Av. Ortiz Rubio and Callejon Libertad s/n, Zona Centro, no tel., Mon.–Fri. 8 A.M.–7 P.M., Sat. 9 A.M.–1 P.M.). Next door is the state tourism office. Continue walking toward the park along Lázaro Cárdenas, and look for the 1941 Iglesia de Nuestra Señora de Guadalupe at the intersection with Avenida Hidalgo. Turn left out of the church and follow Avenida Hidalgo to Calle Elías Calles, where you'll find the Tecate Brewery. Back on Elías Calles, turn right to follow the railroad tracks to the Old Tecate Railroad Station. The tour concludes back at the park.

Rancho La Puerta

Aside from its beer, Tecate is known the world over for its exclusive fitness resort and spa, Rancho La Puerta (U.S. tel. 760/744-4222 or toll-free U.S. tel. 800/443-7565, www.rancholapuerta.com). Founded in the 1940s at the base of Mount Cuchumá/Kuchumaa, the resort has hosted the likes of Madonna, Steven Seagal, Jodie Foster, and Oprah Winfrey. Well ahead of their time, the resort's founders advocated a simple and health-oriented retreat in a beautiful natural setting as an antidote to the busy modern lifestyle. Participants come for a week at a time to hike in the sierra, soak in the hot springs, learn to cook new foods, and enjoy eating fresh produce from the organic farm.

The addition of the **Saturdays at the Ranch** program has opened the resort up to a wider audience. These one-day visits include fitness, spa, and culinary components, all packed into a single 12-hour day that begins and ends in San Diego (tel. 665/654-9155, U.S. tel. 800/443-7565, 8 A.M.–8 P.M., US$195 pp, spa treatments cost extra).

ENTERTAINMENT AND EVENTS

Nightlife is virtually non-existent in Tecate, but in the daytime, off-road races provide a popular pastime for locals and visitors alike. The Santa Veronica Offroad Park and Roadway (www.ranchosantaveronica.com, haciendasantaveronica@hotmail.com), at Rancho Santa Veronica, 30 kilometers east of Tecate off Mexico 2, produces a few such events each year, including the **Gran Carrera de Tecate,** a three-day festival held in late May. The **Gran Carrera de Caballos** is more popular among locals. It takes place on the last weekend in March.

The **SCORE Tecate Baja 500** occurs in June and early November (U.S. tel. 818/225-8402).

During the second week of October, the city celebrates the **Fiesta de la Fundación de Tecate,** which commemorates Tecate's founding in a multiday festival of parades, live music, and (rare in Baja) fireworks.

SHOPPING

There are a few shops near the plaza, but the best place to browse for souvenirs is the **Centro de Artesanías de Tecate** (Calzada Universidad near Parque Adolfo López Mateos, Mon.–Fri. 8:30 A.M.–6 P.M., Sat. 10 A.M.–3 P.M.). Originally a workshop for glassblowing, the center sells a full range of pottery, jewelry, and other crafts.

ACCOMMODATIONS AND CAMPING
Hotels and Motels
UNDER US$50

Hotel Tecate (Cardenas y Callejón Libertad No. 20, tel. 665/654-1116, US$35) has 12 simple rooms, but only a few had TVs at last check. The rooms that overlook the plaza have better lighting.

Centrally located **El Paraíso** (Aldrete 83 at Av. Juárez, tel. 665/654-1716, US$25 pp) has 38 clean rooms with air-conditioning and hot showers. The management also provides space heaters for chilly winter nights. There is secure parking in an underground garage.

La Hacienda (Av. Juárez 861, tel. 665/654-1250, US$40) offers clean and safe accommodations on the outskirts of town. Rooms have air-conditioning and cable TV, and there is secure parking. It has a restaurant that's open 8 A.M.–4 P.M. daily, except for Monday when it closes at noon. A cab ride to the town center costs about US$5.

US$50-100

Two blocks west of the Paraíso, **El Dorado** (Av. Juárez 160, tel. 665/654-1333, eldorado@yahoo.com.mx, US$57) is a non-descript two-story motel on the west side of town at Avenida Juárez and Calle Esteban. Its large rooms have air-conditioning, heat, TV, and phone. Off-street parking is available.

On the road to Ensenada, just outside of town, the **Hotel Rosita Resort Inn** (Km 3.6, Carr. Tecate-Ensenada, tel. 665/103-0093, www.rositaresortinn.com.mx, US$50–100) has 52 rooms and suites with modern amenities like air-conditioning, phone, cable TV, and high-speed Internet. Its restaurant serves Mexican specialties, and the recreation area has a swimming pool. Secure parking is another feature.

Ranch Resorts

Popular with the ATV and motorcycle crowds, **Hacienda Santa Verónica** (Km 95, Carr. Tijuana-Mexicali Cuota/Mexico 2-D, tel. 665/521-0017 or -0018, U.S. tel. 888/556-6288, www.ranchosantaveronica.com, US$70) is located about 30 kilometers east of Tecate. Mission-style accommodations (52 rooms and 8 suites) have fireplaces and patios, and meal plans are an option. Activities include tennis, off-road riding (quad rentals US$40/hr), horseback riding, swimming, volleyball, and basketball, and you can come for just the day (8 A.M.–10:30 P.M.) Its campground/RV park is open to the public. To find the resort, exit at Km 106 from the free road and follow the signs; there is no exit for the ranch from the toll road.

Rancho Los Chabacanos (Km. 118 Carr. Mexicali-Tecate, tel. 665/655-1624, U.S.

tel. 619/565-1183, www.rancholoschabacanos. com, US$95–285) has a distinct colonial feel in both its hacienda-style architecture and the surrounding eco-preserve. There are no TVs or phones in its 17 casitas, though Wi-Fi is an option. Guests enjoy black mud treatments and steam treatments in the on-site spa.

Stays at **Rancho La Puerta** (U.S. tel. 760/744-4222 or toll-free U.S. tel. 800/443-7565, www.rancholapuerta.com) are a full week, and include all meals. Accommodations are in cottages or suites—most with fireplaces and each with its own private garden—and the resort can hold 150 guests at a time. Organic produce comes from the resort's own farm.

All-inclusive prices range from US$2,780 per week for a studio with bath to US$4,205 for a two-bedroom villa suite. Summer rates (late June–early September) are lower.

Camping and RV Parks

Rancho Ojai (tel. 665/655-3014, www.rancho-ojai.com) offers cabins, RV sites with full hook-ups, and cabins on their working ranch. This is a family-friendly place that is popular with up-scale Tijuana and Tecate residents, who come for the immaculate cabins, pool, and miniature golf. Rancho Ojai is part of the KOA network, and has been voted one of top KOA campgrounds in the world. Cabins with shared bath are US$68, US$90 with private bath, and US$135 with private bath and kitchenette. The ranch is 21 kilometers east of Tecate on Mexico 2. Exit the toll road at El Hongo and drive west on Mexico 2 for eight kilometers to the Rancho Ojai gates.

Rancho Santa Verónica (30 km east of Tecate at Km 98, Mexico 2, U.S. tel. 888/556-6288, haciendasantaveronica@hotmail.com, www.ranchosantaveronica.com, US$20) also has full-hookup slots and tent spaces. Guests may use any of the ranch's recreational facilities.

FOOD

There is no better place in Baja to try your first real tacos than the stands near Tecate's Hidalgo Park. Each one does this Mexican standard a little differently; Mexicans tend to eat tacos for their evening meal, but the taquerías are usually open from late morning until late in the evening. **Taquería Los Amigos** (Callejón Libertad and Rubio, no tel.) is one of the busiest, and the carne asada in particular is excellent.

For a place where the people-watching can be better than the food (and the food is good), try **☾ El Jardín TKT (Tecate)** (no tel., daily 6 A.M.–noon, mains under US$10) located on the south side of the plaza. They serve inexpensive Mexican standards for breakfast, lunch, and dinner. Outside seating is available during warm weather. The chile verde is excellent.

Mariscos Victor (Av. Hidalgo 284, no tel., from 7 A.M. for breakfast, lunch, and dinner, mains US$5–10) makes dependable seafood dishes and ranch-style entrées like *machaca* and *bistek*.

With a history dating back to 1969, **☾ El Mejor Pan de Tecate** (Av. Juárez 331, btw Rodríguez/Portes Gil, tel. 665/654-0040, www.elmejorpandetecate.com) has impressed many a visitor with its handmade brick-oven breads—some of the best you'll find anywhere in Baja.

Groceries

Several *tiendas* on Avenida Juárez and Avenida Hidalgo stock the basics; a **Calimax** supermarket on Avenida Juárez near the Calle Carranza intersection has more selection.

INFORMATION AND SERVICES
Tourist Assistance

The **Secretaría de Turismo** (Secretary of Tourism or SECTUR, tel. 665/654-1095, www.tecatemexico.com.mx, Mon.–Fri. 9 A.M.–7 P.M., Sat. 9 A.M.–3 P.M., Sun. 10 A.M.–2 P.M.) is located on the south side of Parque Hidalgo, next door to the police station. Or stop by the smaller booth at the border crossing (Lázaro Cárdenas and Madero).

Money

Most places in Tecate accept U.S. currency. There's a money exchange in Tecate,

© PABLO NOBILI

a typical shoe-shine stand in downtown Tecate

California, in the same plaza as the U.S. post office and Western Union.

The Banamex on Avenida Juárez and Serfín on Calle Cárdenas both have ATMs and currency exchange services.

Post Office

Tecate's post office is on the corner of Calles Madero and Ortiz Rubio.

Immigration and Customs

The immigration and customs offices at the border crossing are open daily 6 A.M.–midnight.

GETTING THERE
By Bus

Tecate's bus depot is on Avenida Juárez at Calle Rodríguez; it has a snack bar and long-distance telephone service. **ABC** (tel. 664/621-2668,

www.abc.com.mx) has regular connections to Mexicali, Tijuana, and Ensenada.

By Car

From San Diego, take I-805 to CA 94 and follow this highway southeast for 66 kilometers to the exit for Tecate. From Arizona, pick up CA 94 from I-8 west. Plan to arrive between 5 A.M.–11 P.M. when the border gate is open.

Be sure to buy a Mexican auto insurance policy online or at the border before you cross into Mexico. Temporary vehicle import permits (required for driving on the mainland, but not in Baja), are issued Monday–Saturday 8 A.M.–4 P.M. at the customs office.

Two Baja, California, state highways pass through Tecate: Mexico 2 (to Tijuana or Mexicali) and Mexico 3 (to Ensenada). The toll road (US$10) between Tijuana and Tecate, Mexico 2-D, parallels the border.

By Rail

The **Pacific Southwest Railway Museum** (State Hwy 94 and Forest Gate Rd., Campo, CA, U.S. weekend tel. 619/478-9937, U.S. weekday tel. 619/465-7776, www.sdrm.org, US$43) offers a periodic rail tour to the Old Tecate Railroad Station (one-day or twilight).

By Foot

For a day trip, you can park in any number of lots on the U.S. side of the border and walk over to Tecate.

MEXICO 3 TO ENSENADA

Mexico 3 is a two-lane state highway that begins in Tecate, follows the foothills of the Sierra Juárez to the Valle del Guadalupe Wine Country, and ends near Ensenada. This route makes a longer, but pleasant alternative to the coastal road from Tijuana.

ENSENADA TO EL ROSARIO

Whether they are on a cruise from Los Angeles, driving from San Diego, or passing through on the way to points south, many travelers find themselves in Ensenada for an afternoon or longer. Those who venture away from the commercial port and busy tourist zone into the town center find a surprisingly pleasant Mexican town to explore.

Beyond the border region but still within easy reach of San Diego, Ensenada has an identity all its own. Cruise ships bring tourists by the thousands. They roam the *malecón* by day and return to their ships at night, leaving the town to the locals and visitors who've driven themselves from the other side of the border for an overnight getaway.

Accordingly, the first few blocks along the busy waterfront are crowded with tourist shops and services. But a few blocks inland, Ensenada transforms into a regional center of commerce with a much more local—and inviting—feel. Ranches, fisheries, and wineries all conduct their business here. Students come to study at several universities. And travelers from mainland Mexico come to explore the wine country in the nearby Valle de Guadalupe. A Dominican mission, Russian colony, and beautiful coastline add to Ensenada's appeal.

South of Ensenada, Mexico 1 meanders through a series of farming communities, including the rolling hills and vineyards of the Valle de Santo Tomás. Legendary sportfishing and surfable waves await all the way south to San Quintín. El Rosario, at the southern end of this region, marks the gateway to the vast central desert and the Valle de los Cirios.

HIGHLIGHTS

(Riviera del Pacífico: For a slice of Ensenada history, walk the grounds of the former Playa Ensenada Hotel and Casino, once run by American boxer Jack Dempsey and now the city's cultural center (page 40).

(La Bufadora: One of the more touristy attractions in Northern Baja, this blowhole is an easy excursion from Ensenada. Visitors congregate around the top of a cavern to watch spumes shoot 30 meters in the air (page 53).

(Ruta del Vino: Taste Mexico's finest vintages at the growing number of boutique wineries in the rural Valle de Guadalupe along Mexico 3 between Ensenada and Tecate (page 55).

(Valle de Santo Tomás: Mexico 1 passes rolling hills carpeted in green, a historic winery, and mission ruins in this grape- and olive-growing region (page 61).

(Parque Nacional Sierra San Pedro Mártir: The tallest peaks on the peninsula offer a refreshing contrast to Baja's desert scenery (page 65).

LOOK FOR (TO FIND RECOMMENDED SIGHTS, ACTIVITIES, DINING, AND LODGING.

Ensenada coastline

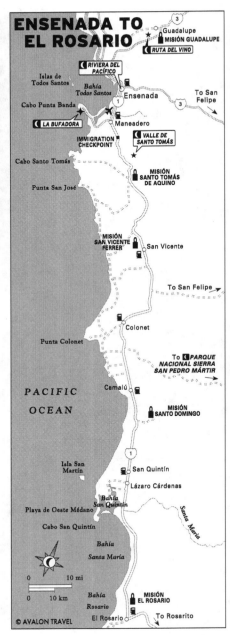

Away from the Pacific coast, hikers and backpackers can explore two mountain ranges, the Sierra Juárez and the Sierra de San Pedro Mártir, which has the tallest peak on the Baja Peninsula, an internationally known observatory, and nearly 69,000 hectares of untouched wilderness.

PLANNING YOUR TIME

Half a day is plenty of time to get a feel for Ensenada. If you have a car, you might spend a few hours or an entire day visiting wineries along the Ruta del Vino. Anglers will be content to spend a week or more plying the waters of Bahía San Quintín.

For sierra-bound visitors, the best hiking seasons are mid-April–mid-June (good for wildflowers) and late September–early November (when quaking aspens put on a show).

Ensenada and Vicinity

More travelers visit Ensenada than any other town on the Baja Peninsula outside of the border region, but this is not a purpose-built resort destination. Thanks to the commercial fishing, aquaculture, and agriculture industries, Ensenada has grown to become the third-largest city in Baja. Farms in the area grow olives and grapes on land, and yellowtail and halibut in the water. Ensenada's port does more business than any other on the peninsula.

Most first-time visitors begin their tour of Ensenada with a stroll along Avenida López Mateos near the waterfront. But if you walk a few blocks away from the harbor, across Avenida Juárez, you'll find yourself in a much quieter, residential part of town with more local-style shops and restaurants.

HISTORY

Spanish explorers Juan Cabrillo (1542) and Sebastián Vizcaíno (1602) were the first Europeans to land at Ensenada, and the first ranches were established through a land grant from Spain in the early 1800s. One of these ranches, Rancho Ensenada, became the inspiration for the town's name. Ensenada experienced dramatic growth when gold was discovered in 1870 and the town transformed into a mining center.

From 1882 to 1915, Ensenada served as the capital city of the Territory of Baja California. U.S. Prohibition fueled another boom in the 1920s, which saw the opening of the historic Ensenada Hotel and Casino, but this time the prosperity was short-lived due to the repeal of Prohibition and the onset of the Great Depression.

In the 1950s, travelers from the United States began visiting Ensenada to take advantage of the sportfishing opportunities, and the city became known as the Yellowtail Capital of the World.

Today, Ensenada is the capital city of the *municipio* (county) of Ensenada, which extends

Ensenada's *malecón* features a giant Mexican flag.

south to the border with Baja California Sur. Around 40,000 expats are permanent residents in the area. The economy is driven by fishing and aquaculture, fish processing, farming, and the import/export trade. The addition of a cruise ship pier and village, plus a scenic *malecón* further enhanced the city's appeal to visitors.

SIGHTS
Riviera del Pacífico

During the U.S. Prohibition era, heavyweight boxing celebrity Jack Dempsey built a massive resort on the Ensenada waterfront called the Playa Ensenada Hotel and Casino. On opening night in 1929, Bing Crosby and the Xavier Cugat Orchestra entertained the crowd. A local singer named Margarita Carmen Cansino joined the orchestra—and later changed her name to Rita Hayworth. A symbol of Ensenada's newfound prosperity, the resort thrived for a few years until the repeal of Prohibition and the onset of the Great Depression sent most of the gamblers home. Management tried reopening the hotel as the

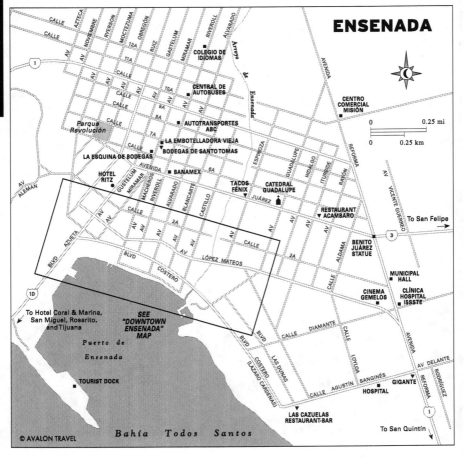

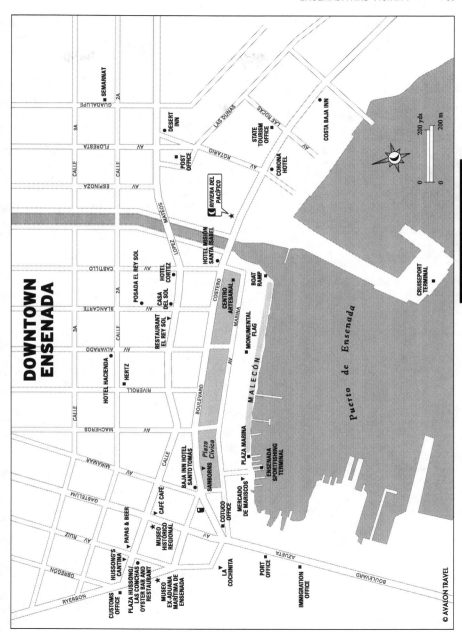

DOWNTOWN ENSENADA

© AVALON TRAVEL

Riviera del Pacífico, but by 1938, the doors had closed for good.

Forty years later, the Mexican government intervened and restored the legendary building as the city's **Centro Social Cívico y Cultural Riviera** (Social, Civic, and Cultural Center, corner of Av. Costero/Riviera). It contains government offices and a public library, as well as a small museum, the **Museo de Historia de Ensenada** (tel. 646/177-0594, Mon.–Sat. 9:30 A.M.–2 P.M. and 3–5 P.M., Sun. 10 A.M.–5 P.M., by donation), with historical exhibits that represent the indigenous people of Baja California, the era of European exploration, and the Dominican missions.

The **Galería de la Cuidad** (tel. 646/177-3130, Mon.–Fri. 9 A.M.–6 P.M.), at the north end of the building, showcases the works of Baja California artists.

Throughout the building, much of the original tile and paintings have been preserved. The street-level **Bar Andaluz** features a mural by Alfredo Ramos Martínez (1871–1946), who established Mexico City's Las Escuelas de Pintura al Aire Libre (Schools of Painting in the Open Air).

Museo Histórico Regional

Ensenada's Museum of Regional History (Av. Gastelum near Av. López Mateos, tel. 646/178-2531, Tues.–Sun. 10 A.M.–5 P.M., by donation) occupies a former 1886 military garrison that housed the Ensenada jail until 1986. The permanent collection consists of native artifacts.

Museo Ex-Aduana Marítima de Ensenada

This historic building downtown was built by the U.S.-based International Land Company of Mexico, which acquired much of the coastline from the Mexican government in the 19th century. Mexico's Aduana Marítima (Maritime Customs) took over in 1922. Then the Instituto Nacional de Antropología e Historia (INAH) stepped in to restore the building and convert it into a museum (Av. Ryerson/Calle Uribe, tel. 646/178-2531, Tues.–Sun. 9 A.M.–4 P.M., by donation). Temporary exhibits cover various Mexican cultural themes.

Malecón

Ensenada's *malecón,* built in the 1990s, is a relatively new fixture on the waterfront. With its giant Mexican flag and bay views, the promenade is a good place to get your bearings before a walk around town. At the north end of the *malecón* are the sportfishing terminal and *mercado de mariscos* (seafood market). Near here, **Plaza Cívica** features statues of three pivotal figures in Mexican history: Benito Juárez (Mexico's first president), Padre Miguel Hidalgo (initiator of the Mexican Revolution), and Venustiano Carranza (first president after the revolution). At the south end, across the narrow Bahía Ensenada, is the cruise ship pier and the Riviera del Pacífico.

Wineries

Ensenada has a long history in the grape-growing/winemaking business and a growing reputation for bottling world-class vintages. Most of the vineyards are located in the nearby Valle de Guadalupe, but several operations have offices and/or tasting rooms in downtown Ensenada.

Bodegas de Santo Tomás (Av. Miramar 666, tel. 646/178-3333, bstwines@hotmail.com, Mon.–Sat. 10 A.M.–9 P.M., Sun. 10 A.M.–5 P.M.) is a good place to get acquainted with the local varietals. As Mexico's oldest winery, its roots go back to the Dominican mission in the Valle de Santo Tomás. The winery offered its first wine to the public in 1888 and moved its winemaking headquarters to Ensenada in 1934. Recently, the company has been shifting its equipment back to Santo Tomás, but the tasting room and wine store in Ensenada remain open to visitors. Short, English-language tours of the facility are available.

SPORTS AND RECREATION
Fishing

Commercial fishing has taken its toll since Ensenada's heyday as a sportfishing getaway in the 1950s and '60s. But a day on a *panga* or cruiser can still yield a decent catch in the peak summer season. Lingcod, rockfish, and bonito are among the most common species.

© PAUL ITOI

Bodegas de Santo Tomás, Mexico's oldest winery

For an old-school fishing experience, hire a *panga* at the Ensenada Sportfishing Terminal near the north end of the harbor or at Punta Banda, south of Ensenada. **Sergio's Sportfishing Center** (tel./fax 646/178-2185, toll-free U.S. tel. 800/336-5454, www.sergiosfishing.com, US$50 pp) is a good choice if you're looking for a six-pack boat. **Gordo's Sportfishing** (tel. 646/178-3515 or 646/178-2377, www.gordossportfishing.com) has larger open party boats and offshore tuna rigs. Be prepared to be badgered by sportfishing salesmen as you walk along the marina to book with any of the outfitters.

Note: By law, anyone who goes out on a fishing boat needs to buy a license, even if you don't plan to fish.

Boating

Marina Coral (radio VHF 71, tel. 646/175-0000, toll-free U.S. tel. 800/862-9020, www.hotelcoral.com), has 500 yacht slips to 135 feet and a floating fuel dock. The marina has a full suite of shore services, including hookups, lockers, restrooms, telephones, and wireless Internet.

Ensenada Cruiseport Village Marina (tel. 646/173-4141, fax 646/173-4151, U.S. tel. 877/219-5822, www.ecpvmarina.com) has 210 slips to 60 feet, LOA and recently renovated laundry and other shore facilities.

As Ensenada is an official Mexican port of entry, arriving boaters must check in with the port captain on Boulevard Azueta. Ensenada's Marina Coral offers the *Ventanilla Unica* (Single Window) service. Boaters can get their tourist cards and TIP (Temporary Import Permits) and pay at the adjoining bank machine. It's open Monday through Friday 8 A.M.–5 P.M.

Surfing

By the time you've reached the surf spots around Ensenada, you've distanced yourself beyond the reach most of the weekend warriors from San Diego. Ensenada has several surf shops located on the north end of town. The **Baja Board Shop** (Loc. 720-4 Costero, Plaza Bocarelli, tel. 646/175-7218, chimbo@hotmail.com) that is often listed as north of town is now located on Boulevard Costero.

San Miguel might be Baja's most consistent point break. It's located just south of the toll booth on Mexico 1. Parking is US$5 and the crowds will be on it if the surf is good. Get there early to catch it before the onshores start up in the late morning. There are several spots as you drive south that are less consistent.

Isla Todos Santos is located 20 kilometers offshore of Ensenada. Killers is located on the northwest side of the island, and breaks on winter swells coming from the northwest. Because of its direct exposure to the north, and a deep water canyon that channels the long period swell, Killers can get huge and is not for the uninitiated. You can hire a boat from the Ensenada harbor for a ride to the island for around US$100.

Diving

There is little shore diving around Ensenada, but boat trips take divers to explore several underwater pinnacles.

Almar Dive Shop (Av. Macheros 149, tel. 646/178-3013, almardive@hotmail.com) offers rental gear and lessons. **Dale's La Bufadora Dive Shop** (Rancho La Bufadora, tel. 646/154-2092, www.labufadoradive.com, open weekends or by appointment) rents gear and does boat trips to the pinnacles just offshore.

Whale-Watching

Sergio's Sportfishing Center (tel./fax 646/178-2185, toll-free U.S. tel. 800/336-5454, www.sergiosfishing.com) and **Gordo's** (tel. 646/178-3515 or 646/178-2377, fax 646/174-04810, www.gordossportfishing.com) offer whale-watching boat tours late December–late March. You won't get as close to the whales here as you can in the gray whale birthing lagoons farther south, but it's still a pleasant way to get out on the water if you're not interested in fishing or diving.

Spa Services

Choose from a variety of treatments and service packages at the spa at **Hotel Coral & Marina** (Km 103 Carr. Tijuana-Ensenada #3421, Zona Playitas, tel. 646/175-0000, toll-free U.S. tel. 800/862-9020, www.hotelcoral.com, Mon.–Sat. 8 A.M.–8 P.M., Sun. 8 A.M.–6 P.M.). Services include Swedish massage, body wraps, and facials.

Cruises

You can visit Ensenada as part of a four-day cruise along the Pacific coast with Royal Caribbean's **Monarch of the Seas** (toll-free U.S. tel. 800/327-6700, www.royalcaribbean. com, US$219–379). The ship departs from Los Angeles. Carnival (www.carnival.com) offers three- and four-day Baja trips aboard the **Paradise** at comparable prices.

Organized Tours

La Jolla, California–based **Baja California Tours** (U.S. tel. 858/454-7166 or toll-free U.S. tel. 800/336-5454, www.bajaspecials.com, bajatours@aol.com, office hours Mon.–Fri. 10 A.M.–4 P.M.) books day trips to Ensenada and the Valle de Guadalupe, as well as points north and south.

ENTERTAINMENT AND EVENTS
Nightlife

Most of the evening entertainment takes place along Avenida López Mateos and Boulevard Costero between Calle Sanginés and Avenida Macheros. Some of the hotels and bars host live music, and there are a few discos, but it's nothing compared to what you'll find in Tijuana.

Ensenada's best-known bar has been serving patrons since 1892. Opened by German immigrant Johan Hussong, ◖ **Hussong's Cantina** (Av. Ruiz 113, tel. 646/178-3210, www.cantinahussongs.com, daily 10 A.M.–1 A.M.) has been a gathering place for expats and locals ever since, and many veteran Baja travelers kick off each road trip down the peninsula with a Tecate, Bohemia, or XX beer here. Late afternoon is the best time to beat the rowdy crowds.

Two-story **Papas and Beer** (Av. Ruiz and López Mateos, tel. 646/174-0145, www.papasandbeer.com, daily noon–3 A.M.), across the street, has less character but is also a little mellower. Next door to Papas, **Oxidos** (Av. Ruiz and López Mateos, tel. 646/178-8827, daily 8 A.M.–midnight) is a lounge-like place with a dance floor.

El Patio (López Mateos 1088, tel. 646/178-3866, www.elpatiobar.com, Mon.–Tues. 6 P.M.–midnight, Wed.–Thurs 1 P.M.–midnight, Fri.–Sat. 1 P.M.–2 A.M., Sun. 1 P.M.–midnight) is the place to sample some high-end tequila and watch the game in a garden patio setting.

Festivals and Events

FEBRUARY

Ensenada puts on a good show for **Carnaval,** during the six days before Ash Wednesday. The festivities include parades, amusement rides, live music, costumes, and lots of food and drink.

APRIL

Thousands of cyclists ride in the **Rosarito-Ensenada 50-Mile Fun Bicycle Ride** (tel. 619/424-6084, www.rosaritoensenada.com) each April. Register online in advance (US$35) or on the day of the event (US$40).

The **Tommy Bahama Newport-Ensenada Race** (www.nosa.org) is a regatta in which hundreds of yachts sail from Southern California to Ensenada.

JUNE

SCORE International and Tecate beer sponsor the annual **Baja 500** (U.S. tel. 818/225-8402, www.score-international.com) off-road race starting in Ensenada.

JULY

Beach volleyball players from all over the world compete for sizable cash prizes in the **Baja Volleyball Open** (www.bajaopen.com) held at Playa Hermosa.

AUGUST

The wine country celebrates the **Fiesta de la Vendimia Bajacaliforniana** (Baja California Wine Harvest Festival, tel. 646/174-0170, www.caniracensenada.com), with 10 days of wine-tasting, winery tours, and gourmet cooking at the wineries around town and in the Valle de Guadalupe. Admission prices vary by location.

SEPTEMBER

J. D. Hussong Baja International Chili Cookoff & Salsa Contest (tel. 646/174-4575, www.hussongs.com/chilicookoff.html, US$10) takes place on a Saturday afternoon at the Quintas Papagayo Resort. Chili connoisseurs battle for the opportunity to attend the annual International Chili Society's World Championship in Omaha, Nebraska. This is one of the most popular events in Ensenada each year.

OCTOBER

The local restaurant association CANIRAC organizes the popular **Feria Internacional del Pescado y el Marisco** (International Seafood Fair, tel. 646/174-0448 or 646/174-0435, www.caniracensenada.com), featuring restaurants from Ensenada and as far away as Tijuana and Southern California.

Pro surfers compete in a two-day **Mexican Surf Fiesta** at Playa de San Miguel (tel. 858/586-9173, www.mexicansurffiesta.com, surfiesta@yahoo.com).

NOVEMBER

The **SCORE-Tecate Baja 1000** (U.S. tel. 818/225-8402, www.score-international.com) off-road race takes over much of the Baja Peninsula for a week each November. On alternate years, the course goes all the way to La Paz. If you happen to be driving Mexico 1 during the week of the race (or the two weeks leading up to it), you'll see clouds of dust following the motorcycles, trucks, and dune buggies that are on the dirt course. And they'll probably be traveling much faster than traffic on the paved highway.

SHOPPING

Ensenada shopping is more international and upscale than what you'll find in Tijuana, a reflection of the sorts of things that cruise ship passengers like to buy. The stores along Avenida

ENSENADA TO EL ROSARIO

© KATHRYN LATENDRESSE

hand-embroidered dresses for sale

López Mateos and Boulevard Costero have an assortment of souvenirs and beachwear. Some of the most popular purchases are silver jewelry, leather goods, pottery, fine art, and accessories for the beach. In general, prices drop the farther you get from the waterfront.

The **Centro Artesanal** (Blvd. Costero 1094 at the end of Av. Castillo) has arts and crafts from all over Mexico.

Open since 1988, **Galería de Pérez Meillón** (Centro Artesanal, Loc. 40, Blvd. Costero 1094 and Av. Castillo, tel. 646/175-7848, adalbertopm@hotmail.com, daily 9 A.M.–5 P.M.) specializes in Mata Ortiz pottery, made by Native Americans from a small village in the mainland state of Chihuahua. Owner Adalberto Pérez Meillón selects each piece directly from the artists. He also carries a variety of other Native American handcrafts, as well as works by contemporary artists living in Baja California and mainland Mexico.

The wide variety of *artesanías* and friendly English-speaking staff create a pleasant shopping experience at **Bazar Casa Ramírez** (Av. López Mateos 496-3, tel. 646/178-8209,

bramirez717@hotmail.com). This large family-run shop contains high-quality crafts from all over Mexico, including Talavera pottery, wrought-iron sculptures, decorative mirrors, and works of carved wood and blown glass. For silver jewelry from Taxco, try **Arriaga de Taxco** (two locations on Avenida López Matéos 821 and 865, tel. 646/174-0704, sterling@telnor.net, Mon.–Fri. 10 A.M.–7 P.M., Sat. until 8 P.M., Sun. until 6 P.M.).

Los Globos (Calle 9 three blocks east of Av. Reforma, daily 9 A.M.–6 P.M.) is a flea market with vendors selling housewares, furniture, apparel, and more. Weekends are best.

For leather goods, try **Nuevo México Lindo** (Av. López Mateos 688, tel. 646/178-1381). It specializes in saddles and related gear but also has handbags.

A few fine art galleries have sprung up around town, including **Galería La Esquina de Bodegas** (Av. Miramar and Calle 6, tel. 646/178-3557, Sun.–Fri. 8 A.M.–10 P.M.), which is located across from Bodegas de Santo Tomás, and shows the works of Mexican and international artists.

Shopping Centers

Ensenada has several large shopping plazas, including **Centro Comercial Misión** (Calle 11 and Av. Reforma), with a Gigante supermarket, Banamex ATM, Lavamática Express, Smart and Final, and Cinema Gemelos.

ACCOMMODATIONS
Downtown

Ensenada's hotels are concentrated along Avenida López Mateos and Boulevard Costero. Late-night noise is a concern here, especially if you end up in a room that faces the street. Also, many of the longtime favorite establishments have let standards slip in recent years to the point where we can no longer recommend them. Aside from peak travel times of July–August, Carnaval (February), and U.S. college spring break (March), hotels are rarely full and rates are negotiable.

The high season in Ensenada is May–September, and weekdays are generally slower than weekends year-round. Rates below do not include 12 percent tax, unless specified. Some places also add a 10 percent service charge to the nightly rate.

UNDER US$50

Hotel Hacienda (Calle 2 #211 at Alvarado, tel. 646/178-2344, US$40) has a good location just one full block from the main drag. Traffic noise is an issue for the rooms that face Calle 2, but all of the rooms are well maintained and clean.

Three blocks north of Hussong's Cantina, **Hotel Ritz** (Av. Ruiz 379 at Calle 4, tel. 646/174-0501, fax 646/178-3262, US$32) appeals to travelers who don't need off-street parking and who prefer to stay a comfortable distance from the main tourist drag (but still within the downtown area). Rooms on the lower level are dark; balconies on the more expensive second and third stories are a nice feature.

US$50-100

The northernmost property in the small **Desert Inn** (Av. Floresta at Bucaneros, tel. 646/176-2601, toll-free U.S. tel. 800/346-3942, www.

desertinns.com, US$70–122) chain of hotels in Baja has 50 rooms in a three-story building. Rooms come with air-conditioning, heat, TV, and phone. There are a restaurant and pool on-site but no off-street parking. It's adequate enough for a place to crash, but certainly nothing special.

Hotel Misión Santa Isabel (Blvd. Costero 1119 btw Av. Castillo/Av. López Mateos, tel. 646/178-3616, fax 646/178-3345, US$39–139) is a large, mission-style building with clean rooms and friendly service—something that seems increasingly hard to find in Ensenada accommodations. Its 57 guestrooms have colonial-style wood furnishings, with modern amenities such as air-conditioning, heat, satellite TV, and direct-dial phones. The welcoming grounds include a restaurant/bar, gift shop, and one of the cleaner swimming pools in town; secure parking is another plus.

Rooms in the mission-style **Casa del Sol Hotel** (Av. López Mateos 1001, tel. 646/178-1570, U.S. tel. 877/316-1684, www.casadel-solmexico.net, US$65–120) come with tiled baths, air-conditioning, TV, phone, and Wi-Fi. Services include secure parking and the on-site Bistro Café Sutaza and Essence Spa, with a full menu of treatments. Your morning coffee is on the house.

Suites are a good value at the **Baja Inn Hotel Santo Tomás** (Blvd. Costero 609 at Av. Miramar, tel. 646/178-1503 or 800/026-6999, toll-free U.S. tel. 800/303-2684, www.bajainn. com, US$80), which is part of the same group of Baja Inn hotels. Its 80 clean rooms have air-conditioning, heat, and satellite TV, and there's secure parking and a restaurant.

US$100-150

The well-run **Hotel Cortez** (Av. López Mateos 1089, tel. 646/178-2307 or 800/026-6999, toll-free U.S. tel. 800/303-2684, www.bajainn. com, US$65–110) has 75 rooms in a two-story colonial-style building with an attractive lobby. Amenities include air-conditioning, heat, direct-dial phones, and cable TV. Nonsmoking rooms are available. The hotel also has a heated pool, restaurant/bar, and secure parking.

US$150-250

The recently renovated five-story, 93-room **(Corona Hotel** (Blvd. Costero 1442, tel. 646/176-0901, www.hotelcorona.com.mx, US$159) gives you an in-town location that's removed from the worst of the noise. Rooms feature bay views, balconies, satellite TV, air-conditioning, and heat. The spa is well appointed and clean. The bar has the feel of a hip ski bar in Switzerland. The secure parking out front can handle any size rig. You can even back your car up to the ground-floor rooms at the front of the hotel.

Popular with the yachting crowd, the **Hotel Coral & Marina** (Km 103, exit Mexico 1 at Ensenada Centro, tel. 646/175-0000, toll-free U.S. tel. 800/862-9020, www.hotelcoral.com, US$150 and up) has a full-service marina in addition to clean and contemporary accommodations. Its suites have balconies overlooking the marina. There is a restaurant serving *alta cocina mexicana,* plus a long list of guest services such as a nightclub, heated indoor and outdoor pools, hot tub, sauna, lighted tennis courts, and parking garage. The place is kid friendly, to boot.

Posada El Rey Sol (Av. Blancarte 130, tel. 646/178-1601, U.S. tel. 888/311-6871, www.posadaelreysol.com, US$80–110) has 52 good-sized rooms, and a heated pool, spa, restaurant, bar, and enclosed parking. It's a block from the waterfront, with a friendly and helpful staff.

Out of Town
US$100-150

Overlooking the Pacific Ocean five kilometers north of town, **Punta Morro Hotel and Suites** (Mexico 1, Km 106, tel. 646/178-3507, toll-free U.S. tel. 800/526-6676, www.punta-morro.com, US$250) has clean and quiet suites, from studios to three-bedroom units. Highlights include well-equipped kitchens, fireplaces, and terraces. The food and spa aren't at the same level as the accommodations, however.

Ocean views are the best part about a night's stay at **Las Rosas Hotel and Spa** (Km. 105.5, Ensenada Road, tel. 646/174-4595 or 866/447-6727, fax 646/175-9031, www.lasrosas.com,

Posada El Rey Sol

© PAUL ITOI

US$150), which is located six kilometers north of town on Mexico 1. The tradeoffs are small baths and no air-conditioning. Amenities include a restaurant with somewhat pricey food, pool, hot tub, sauna, exercise center, and tennis court.

OVER US$250

At the highest end of the spectrum, **(Casa Natalie** (Km 103.3, tel. 646/174-7373, toll-free U.S. tel. 800/562-8254, www.casanatalie.com, US$180–395), located near the Hotel Coral & Marina has five suites furnished to a level rarely seen in Baja. Three more rooms opened in 2007. If you can drag yourself away from the infinity pool, this would be the ideal home base for a weekend of wine tasting in the Guadalupe Valley.

FOOD

Fish tacos and seafood cocktails top the list of foods to try in Ensenada (or anywhere in coastal Baja, for that matter). One of the best places to try these local delights is the **(Mercado de Mariscos** (Seafood Market, Blvd. Costero at Av. Miramar, daily late morning–early evening), behind the Plaza Marina on the waterfront. You can also buy fresh fish here to cook yourself.

Mexican

(Manzanilla (Blvd Teniente Azueta 139, tel. 646/175-7073, www.rmanzanilla.com, Wed.–Sat. noon–midnight, US$10–30) has become one of Ensenada's top restaurants. Guests are greeted by the co-owner, and the restaurant is known for its rib eye, raw fish, and local wines. The restaurant uses local organic ingredients and seafood.

Rinconcito Oaxaqueño (no tel., daily 9 A.M.–5 P.M.), off Diamante and a block south of Reforma, serves authentic Oaxacan cuisine. You can order nopales, *chicharron,* or carne asada in a taco or plate from US$1–5. If they are in season, and you're an adventurous eater, try the grasshoppers (*chapulines*) washed down with an ice cold Dos Equis.

Acambaro (El Refugio Ensenadense) (Av.

MEXICAN-STYLE EGGS

Mexican-style egg-and-beans plates come in many different styles. They typically are served as a late breakfast or brunch on weekends and holidays. Here are some of the preparations you may see on the menu:

- *huevos revueltos:* scrambled eggs

- *huevos duros:* hard-boiled eggs

- *huevos escafaldos:* soft-boiled eggs

- *huevos estrellados:* eggs fried sunny side up

- *huevos a la Mexicana/huevos mexicanos:* eggs scrambled with chopped tomato, onion, and chilies

- *huevos rancheros:* fried eggs served on a tortilla

- *huevos divorciados:* two *huevos estrellados* separated by beans, each egg usually topped with a different salsa

- *con chorizo:* with ground sausage

- *con machaca:* with dried, shredded meat

- *con tocino:* with bacon

- *con jamón:* with ham

Iturbide 528 off Av. Juárez btw Calles 5/6, tel. 646/176-5235, daily for breakfast, lunch, and dinner, mains US$10–15) serves tasty Mexican dishes in a rustic wood and brick setting. Plates arrive with the works: limes, oregano, and salsa.

A group of restaurants along Avenida Lópes Mateos specializes in roast chickens: **Hacienda del Charro** (Av. López Mateos 454, tel. 646/178-2114, daily for lunch and dinner till 11:30 P.M.) is the best one along this strip, also offering chicken tamales and *pollo pipián* (chicken cooked in a pumpkin-seed mole). The tangy flavor of homemade *agua de jamaica* (hibiscus) balances the savory chicken.

Las Cazuelas Restaurant Bar (Sanginés 6 near Blvd. Costero, tel. 646/176-1044, daily 7 A.M.–11 P.M., mains US$10–25) is an old standby serving border-style cuisine, including *codorniz* (quail), seafood, steaks, ribs, and hearty Mexican breakfasts.

The most unique food experience in Ensenada is still offered at **€ El Taco de Huitzilopochtli** (Av. de las Rosas 5, Col. Valle Verde, tel. 646/174-2381, Sat.–Sun. 9 A.M.–5 P.M., mains under US$10). The house specialty is *mixiote,* which is lamb wrapped in maguey leaves and then baked for 16 hours in a wood-fired oven. They start the process on Friday, and the food isn't ready until Saturday morning. The menu is limited only by your sense of adventure. You can order *huitlacoche* (corn fungus tacos) or *huanzontle,* a reedy vegetable. The easiest way to get there is to take a taxi from downtown, and you'll appreciate not having to drive if you're there when the owner breaks out the "house" tequila.

On the corner of Espinoza and Juarez, **Tacos Fénix** (daily noon–8 P.M.) serves up some of the town's best seafood tacos out of a stand across from the Calimax. Shrimp tacos are light and crispy, and they cost US$1–1.50 each.

Seafood

Las Conchas Oyster Bar and Restaurant (tel. 646/175-7375, daily for lunch and dinner, mains US$15 and up), in Plaza Hussong, draws a crowd for oysters *(ostiones)* and other seafood specialties. It's a popular place, so expect to wait for a table.

Tacos el Fenix (Av. Espinosa at Av. Juárez, no tel., daily 8 A.M.–8 P.M.) prepares fish and prawn tacos for US$1 each.

Asian

La Cochinita (Paseo Hidalgo next to Maritime Customs, tel. 646/178-5445, www.lacochinita.com.mx, daily lunch and dinner) is a Baja chain that specializes in Mexican-style Japanese food. There are a dozen locations in Ensenada and more in major cities throughout the peninsula.

the happy meeting of corn and flour at a local *tortillería*
© CARMEL TSABAR

Cafés

Stop in for a quick bite at **El Faro Café** (no tel., mains under US$10), before a day of sportfishing. Located next to Gordo's Sportfishing, behind Plaza Marina on the waterfront, it opens early at 4:30 A.M. and serves breakfast only.

Pueblo Café Deli (Av. Ruiz 96, tel. 646/178-8055, daily 8 A.M.–midnight) serves espresso drinks, plus breakfast foods, Mexican fare, salads, pastries, wine, and beer.

Dependable **Sanborns Café** (Plaza Marina, Blvd. Costero, tel. 646/174-0971, daily 7:30 A.M.–10 P.M., mains US$10–15) always has a number of soups, salads, sandwiches, breakfasts, and Mexican dishes on the menu.

Café Café (Av. López Mateos 496, tel. 646/178-8209, daily from 9 A.M.) is a combination coffee house/art gallery that also hosts occasional cultural events and performances.

European

El Rey Sol (Av. López Mateos 1000 at Av. Blancarte, tel. 646/178-1733, daily 7:30 A.M.–10:30 P.M., mains US$20 and up) is an Ensenada institution for fine French cuisine. The restaurant was founded in 1947 by a native of Santa Rosalía (a town in southern Baja that was built by a French mining company) named Doña Pepita, who studied at the Cordon Bleu cooking school in France. Whether you choose a seafood, poultry, or meat entrée, it will arrive with fresh herbs and vegetables from the family's ranch in the Valle de Santo Tomás, south of Ensenada.

In the Bodegas de Santo Tomás building, **La Embotelladora Vieja** (Av. Miramar 666 at Calle 7, tel. 646/174-0807, Mon. and Wed. noon–11 P.M., Thurs.–Sat. noon–11 P.M., Sun. noon–5 P.M., mains US$20 and up), has a Mediterranean menu and an international wine list.

Groceries

The **Gigante** at Avenidas Reforma and Delante is the largest supermarket in town and the easiest to find on your way through. Stop here to pick up just about anything you left behind at home.

Avenida Diamante has a string of local *panaderías, tortillerías,* and *dulcerías.* Vendors along the highway south of town sell fresh tamales, as well as local olives, chilies, and honey.

INFORMATION AND SERVICES
Tourist Assistance

The **Baja California State Tourism Secretariat** (Blvd. Costero and Calle Las Rocas, tel. 646/172-3022, Mon.–Fri. 8 A.M.–5 P.M., Sat.–Sun. 10 A.M.–3 P.M.) has a wealth of information regarding local events, restaurants, and accommodations, as well as for the entire state. The staff speaks English and will be happy to help.

The **Ensenada Tourism Trust** (Blvd. Lázaro Cárdenas 609-5, tel. 646/178-8578 or 800/025-3991, toll-free U.S. tel. 800/310-9687, www.enjoyensenada.com) has much of the same information.

Money

There are several ATMs in town, including a Banamex at Avenida Juárez and Riveroll and a

---

ENSENADA PHONE NUMBERS

- Ensenada area code: 646
- Customs: 174-0897
- Fire Department: 068
- Green Angels: 176-4675
- Highway Patrol: 176-1311
- Immigration: 174-0164
- IMSS Hospital: 172-4500
- ISSSTE Hospital: 176-5276
- Police: 060
- Red Cross: 066
- State Police: 061
- State Tourism Office: 172-3022
- Tourist Assistance: 078

ENSENADA TO EL ROSARIO

Banca Serfín at Avenida Ruiz 290. Most banks in Ensenada refer visitors to a *casa de cambio* for foreign-exchange services. Several shopping centers along Avenida Juárez and Avenida Reforma feature money-changing booths or storefronts.

Post and Telephone

There is a post office at the corner of Avenidas López Mateos and Rotario (Riviera), across from the Desert Inn (Mon.–Fri. 8 A.M.–6 P.M., Sat. 9 A.M.–1 P.M.). Public telephones are a better deal for local and long-distance calls than hotel phones.

Immigration

If you plan to travel south of Maneadero and haven't validated your tourist card yet, you'll need to pay a visit to the Ensenada immigration office (tel. 646/174-0164, daily 9 A.M.–5 P.M.), next to the port captain's office (COTP) on Avenida Azueta. Look for the turnoff near the waterfront at the northern entrance into town.

Parking here can be a challenge, since there is no public lot for the office, and most of the curbs nearby are painted red. Consider parking farther away and walking in.

If you run into any problems getting your tourist permit here, go to the state tourism office (Blvd. Costero and Calle Las Rocas, tel. 646/172-3022) and ask for help from the SECTUR *delegado*.

Language Schools

Colegio de Idiomas de Baja California (Baja California Language College, Av. Riveroll 1287, tel. 646/174-1741, U.S. tel. 619/758-9711 or 877/444-2252, www.bajacal.com) teaches 30-hour Spanish classes for US$279. Classes are small groups and courses take one week to complete.

The **Center of Languages and Latin American Studies** (Calle Felipe Angeles #15, tel. 646/178-7600, www.spanishschoolbaja.com) also has a one-week program (US$280), with discounts for four or more weeks. Materials, homestays, meals, and registration cost extra.

Emergencies

The **Clínica Hospital ISSSTE** (Calle Sanginés and Av. Pedro Loyola, tel. 646/176-5276) offers 24/7 emergency medical services. For ambulance service, call **Cruz Roja** (tel. 066). If you need emergency treatment at San Diego medical facilities, contact **TransMedic Ambulance** (842-3 Av. Ruiz, tel. 646/178-1400), a 24/7 emergency service that offers air and land transportation to San Diego.

GETTING THERE
By Air

Ensenada's **Aeropuerto El Ciprés** (tel. 646/177-4503) is located three kilometers south of town off Mexico 1. It is a military base and an official Mexican airport of entry with a paved airstrip; however, only two regional airlines currently offer regular service. If you aren't flying your own plane or travel to and from Guerrero Negro or Isla Cedros, this airport isn't going to be of much use.

By Bus

Autotransportes de Baja California (ABC) offers intercity connections on air-conditioned buses, departing from the Central de Autobuses terminal at Avenida Riveroll and Calle 11 (tel. 646/178-6680). Buses leave this terminal twice a day for points south, including San Quintín (4 hours), Guerrero Negro (8 hours), Santa Rosalía (12 hours), Loreto (15 hours), and La Paz (20 hours).

Buses without air conditioning leave from the smaller terminal at Avenida Riveroll and Calle 8 (tel. 646/177-0909, every hour to Tijuana from 5 A.M.–9:30 P.M.).

The **Transportes Norte de Sonora** (TNS, Tijuana tel. 664/688-1979) and **Estrellas de Oro** (Tijuana, tel. 664/683-5022) companies all offer connection to Guaymas, Los Mochis, Mazatlán, Guadalajara, and Mexico City on the mainland.

By Car

Ensenada marks the end of the toll road, Mexico 1-D, from Tijuana. From here until Los Cabos, Mexico 1 is a paved, two-lane highway that's narrow and without a shoulder for much of its length.

Mexico 3 from Tecate also passes through Ensenada on its way to the Sierra Juárez and the intersection with Mexico 5 near San Felipe. Here's how to pick up Mexico 3 heading east out of Ensenada: Take Avenida Juárez to Avenida Reforma at the Benito Juárez statue. Cross Avenida Reforma and follow the street called Calzada Cortés until it turns left and becomes Mexico 3.

GETTING AROUND
By Bus

Ensenada's compact tourism zone can be managed by foot, but a number of public buses do run along the main streets (US$0.50). The route is usually given as a street name posted in the window.

By Taxi

Taxis can be found along Avenidas López Mateos or Juárez, and at the bus depot on Calle

11 at Avenida Riveroll. Trips within the city should cost under US$10. Negotiate the fare before you get in. A taxi ride to La Bufadora costs US$10–15.

By Car and Motor Scooter
RENTAL CARS AND MOTOR SCOOTERS
Since it doesn't have an international airport, Ensenada has less demand for rental cars, and fewer agencies means higher prices. Most visitors either drive their own car, take the bus, or rent a car in San Diego. Only a few of the major chains still allow cars to be driven into Mexico (Avis and Hertz are two that do; you'll have to buy Mexican auto insurance when you pick up the vehicle at the San Diego airport). **Fiesta Rent-A-Car** (Blvd. Costero 1442, in the lobby of Hotel Corona, tel. 646/176-3344) is one local option. If you don't mind prepaying and not knowing which company you will rent from, you can also book a car through a discount service like HotWire. com. Rates at press time started at US$35 per day (without Mexican auto insurance).

At the south end of Plaza Cívica, **Chavo's Sport Rentals** (Gaviotas #256, tel. 646/212-7677 or 646/201-5942) rents Yamaha motor scooters and ATVs for around US$20 per hour.

DRIVING
Ensenada is a big city with busy streets, but it's not impossible to navigate. Just take your time, watch for signs, and stop at every intersection, whether you see a stop sign or not. Absolutely do not speed or drink while driving.

ESTERO BEACH
Twelve kilometers south of Ensenada, the Río San Carlos meets Bahía de Todos Santos to form an estuary environment. The beach here isn't the prettiest that Baja has to offer (unless you're into tidal flats), but it tends not to be too crowded, except in the middle of the summer. Turn off Mexico 1 7.5 kilometers south of the Gigante at Avenidas Reforma and Delante.

Accommodations
There are a few motels near the beach, but the Estero Beach Resort or its attached RV park are the best options if you want to spend the night. The well-worn and family-oriented **Estero Beach Resort Hotel** (Km 14, Carretera Transpeninsular, tel. 646/176-6225 or 646/176-6230, U.S. tel. 619/335-1145, www.hotelesterobeach.com, US$80–120) has 100 rooms and suites, most of which have views of the beach and are set amidst landscaped grounds of grass and palms. This is a full-service resort, but think Super 8 more than Crowne Plaza, and you'll be pleasantly surprised. Families who fall in love with the place tend to return every year until their kids are grown. Guest services include tennis courts, boat rentals, horseback riding, a swimming pool, playground, restaurant/bar, general store, and small historical museum. The adjoining RV park has 60 spaces with full hookups and grassy campsites (US$35–45). This place is popular with caravans, so book early. Campers are allowed to use the hotel facilities. There are several less expensive campgrounds and trailer parks along the beach.

Getting There
City buses signed for the Chapultepec neighborhood run between downtown Ensenada and the estuary.

PUNTA BANDA
The estuary at the south end of Bahía Todos Santos is protected by a sharp, rocky peninsula that extends northwest and ends at a cape called Cabo Banda. The name Punta Banda is used to reference the peninsula, the cape, and a settlement on the bay.

A large-scale real estate development is scheduled to open in 2011 with 100 villas and 40 home sites, starting at US$3 million. The par-70 golf course will be closed to the public, so if you want to play the Tiger Woods–designed course, you'll need to pony up for a home site or be invited by someone who has.

◖ La Bufadora
If you miss the chance to see gray whales spouting offshore Punta Banda, this blowhole on the south side of the peninsula is

not a bad substitute. A frequent stop on the tour bus circuit—and popular with locals as well—La Bufadora (The Snorter) creates a spectacular display as incoming swells push seawater into an underground canyon and out through a hole in the rocks. The resulting explosion of water and spray reaches heights of 25–30 meters. The sight has been developed with a small visitor center and restrooms. A number of food vendors line the road to the parking area.

Water Sports

Dale's La Bufadora Dive Shop (Rancho La Bufadora, tel. 646/154-2092, www.labufadoradive.com, open weekends or by appointment) is a multi-sport operation on tiny Bahía Papalote that offers *panga* fishing (US$35 per person, min. two people), unguided dive trips (US$35 per person, min. two people), and kayak rentals (US$20 per half-day, US$30 per full-day).

La Bufadora is an excellent place to begin a scuba diving tour of the Baja Peninsula if you don't mind cold water. Its pinnacles, kelp beds, and giant green anemones make for memorable dives. Conditions in the bay are best for intermediate to advanced divers, as there is a good amount of surge except on the calmest of days. Currents keep the water here a few degrees colder than temperatures in San Diego. You'll need lots of neoprene or, preferably, a dry suit to be comfortable. You can rent gear and reserve a boat from Dale's, or through the Almar dive shop in Ensenada (Av. Macheros 149, tel. 646/178-3013, almardive@hotmail.com).

Another option for fishing is **Vonny's Fleet** (tel. 646/154-2046, www.vonnysfleet.com, U$139/boat up to three people), which launches *pangas* from the beach at Punta Banda.

Camping and RV Parks

La Jolla Beach Camp (Km 12.5 BCN 23, La Jolla, tel. 646/154-2005, US$15) is a large, basic park that faces Bahía de Todos Santos. Its 200 sites come with use of hot showers, boat ramp, tennis court, and dump station (no hookups, except for a few sites with electricity). The park also has its own market and restaurant.

Next door, smaller **Villarino RV Park** (Km 13 BCN 23, La Jolla, Ensenada, tel. 646/154-2004, US$22–28) has a little more character, plus some of its sites have full hookups. The park has clean restrooms, hot showers, picnic tables, a boat ramp, boat rentals, restaurant, and market. The office is open daily 9 A.M.–noon and 1–5 P.M.

Three *ejido*-run campgrounds on the peninsula have restrooms and water, but no other facilities (US$5).

You can walk to Dale's La Bufadora Dive Shop from **Rancho La Bufadora** (tel. 646/178-7172, US$15), which overlooks Bahía Papalote. It has primitive campsites, and there are flush toilets and 24/7 security.

Getting There

To get to Punta Banda from Ensenada by car, follow Mexico 1 about 25 kilometers south to BCN 23, a right turn that comes before Maneadero. Take this road west through the retirement community of La Jolla and along the peninsula. The road will climb over the rocks and around to south-facing La Bufadora. A taxi ride from Ensenada to La Bufadora runs about US$15–20.

Valle de Guadalupe

The scenic Guadalupe Valley follows the Río Guadalupe between Ensenada and Tecate on Mexico 3, with a small town at Km 77.

MISIÓN NUESTRA SEÑORA DE GUADALUPE DEL NORTE

Padre Félix Caballero established the last of nine Dominican missions (1834–1840) in Baja in 1834, 24 kilometers east of the next closest mission (San Miguel), above the Río Guadalupe. The missions were already on the decline at this point, but the new settlement became a successful farm and ranch with 400 indigenous people under its tutelage, if only for a few short years. The mission ruins are not recognizable today.

COLONIA RUSA

After the Mexican government secularized the mission properties, a group of Russian pacifists called the Molokans (milk-drinkers, who abstained from drinking alcohol), fled the Russian Orthodox Church and purchased the land surrounding this settlement to start a new colony in 1905.

The original families planted crops and vineyards, raised livestock, built adobe houses, and went about their simple way of life.

In 1938, then-president Cárdenas seized all foreign-owned property in the country, and 3,000 Mexicans arrived to take over the colony, renaming it Francisco Zarco. Only a few of the original Russian families stayed in the area, but the area retains a Russian look and feel. Some of the Molokan homes have survived the years, and tombstones in the town cemetery have Russian enscriptions.

The neighboring **Museo Comunitario del Valle de Guadalupe** (Tues.–Sun. 10 A.M.–6 P.M., by donation) and **Museo Histórico del Valle de Guadalupe** (Tues.–Sun. 10 A.M.–5 P.M., by donation) display historical artifacts, such as clothing, photos, and tools. To find the cemetery (across from the Monte Xanic winery) and museums, turn off the highway at Francisco Zarco and follow the paved road to its end. Turn right and go another 150 meters.

❰ RUTA DEL VINO

The Valle de Guadalupe is an internationally recognized winemaking region that has been gaining attention from Southern California residents and the U.S. travel press in recent years. Baja California wines are shipped all over Mexico and Western Europe, but because of U.S. and Canadian trade policies, they weren't exported north of the border until recent years. They're still difficult to find in Canada and the United States.

The highest concentration of wineries—more than two-dozen at last count—are located in the 23-kilometer-long Valle de Guadalupe, located off Mexico 3, northeast of Ensenada. The introduction of stainless steel tanks and temperature-controlled barrels at many of these vineyards have helped put Baja wines on the map. But you can still enjoy personal service and, often, time with the winemakers themselves as you make your way through the valley. Spring and summer are the most popular time to visit, though Mexican holiday weekends also draw a crowd.

You might start your tour at the west end of Guadalupe Valley in the village of San Antonio de las Minas. At **Vinisterra** (Km 94.5, tel. 646/178-3350, www.vinisterra.com, Sat. 11 A.M.–4:30 P.M., Sun. 11 A.M.–3 P.M.), Abelardo and Patricia Macouzet Rodriguez offer a cabernet sauvignon–merlot blend, tempranillo, and other award-winning wines.

Inquire about the award-winning merlot at family-owned **Viña de Liceaga** (Km 93.5, tel. 646/155-3091, www.vinosliceaga.com, Mon.–Fri. 8 A.M.–3 P.M., Sat.–Sun. 11 A.M.–3 P.M.). Choose from several tasting options for US$3–5. Reservations are recommended. Nearby, contemporary **Casa de Piedra** (Km 93.5, tel. 646/155-3097, www.vinoscasadepiedra. com) offers tastings in a farmhouse setting.

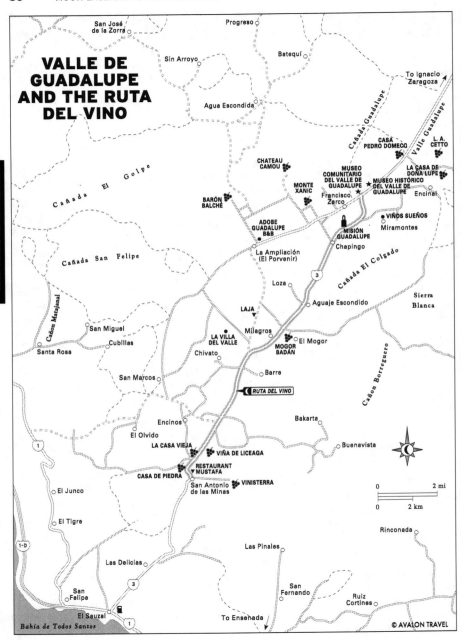

BAJA CALIFORNIA'S WINE TIMELINE

Though it's a relatively new phenomenon to many foreign wine connoisseurs, Baja California's wine history dates back several centuries.

- **Early 16th century:** Hernán Cortés introduces Spanish vines to Mexico.

- **1597:** The Jesuits set up a winery in the present-day state of Coahuila.

- **1697:** Padre Juan Ugarte transplants the cuttings to Misión San Javier.

- **1791:** Dominican Padre José Lorieto establishes Misión Santo Tomás de Aquino, introducing the first vines of Spanish origin to the Valle de Santo Tomás, 45 kilometers south of Ensenada.

- **1888:** Italian miner Francisco Andronequi assumes control of the former mission vineyard and renames it Bodegas de Santo Tomás.

- **1906:** A Russian Christian sect acquires a tract of land in the Valle de Guadalupe and plants more vineyards, which prove to grow exceptionally well in the hot, dry Baja climate.

- **1939:** A former general from the Mexican Revolution, Abelardo Lujan Rodríguez, buys Bodegas de Santo Tomás and moves its headquarters north to Ensenada.

- **Early 1960s:** Rodríguez hires a winemaker from the internationally renowned school for viticulture and oenology at the University of California at Davis, who introduces new varietals as well as modern winemaking technology.

- **1972:** Pedro Domecq, a maker of brandy from Spain, establishes a wine-making operation in the Valle de Guadalupe, creating a buzz for Baja wines within the international wine community.

- **1990s:** Boutique wineries including Monte Xanic and Chateau de Camou (Viñas de Camou) raise the bar even higher, establishing credibility and visibility for the emerging wine region.

- **2007:** Baja California wineries account for approximately 90 percent of all wine made in the country.

Reservations are required. Once a year, it offers a four-weekend wine-making seminar. **La Casa Vieja** (Km 93.5, tel. 646/155-3153, lacasavieja.baja@hotmail.com) opens daily at 9 A.M. and closes at sunset, or whenever the crowd disperses. In addition to offering tastings, this winery has a deli, arts and crafts store, and information center on-site.

Chateau Camou (tel. 646/177-2221 or 646/177-3303, www.chateau-camou.com.mx, Mon.–Sat. 8 A.M.–3 P.M., Sun. 9 A.M.–2 P.M.) specializes in expensive Bordeaux-style reds. It offers three tasting/tour options: Try four wines and a tour for US$5, six tastings and a tour for US$10, or a tour with the winemaker and a complete tasting including a barrel sample for US$40.

Next up, **Mogor Badán** (Km 86.5, tel. 646/177-1484, abadan@cicese.mx) is a combination organic produce farm, vineyard, and winery with tours, tastings, and shopping. Reservations are required. Baja's most acclaimed winery, **Monte Xanic** (tel. 646/174-7055, www.montexanic.com, Mon.–Fri. 9 A.M.–4 P.M., Sat. 8 A.M.–noon), produces 50,000 cases of wine per year, and many of its labels have won awards in the United States, Canada, and Mexico. The winery charges US$4 for tasting whites and an additional US$4 for reds. Reservations are required.

Housed in an adobe brick building, **Barón Balché** (El Porvenir, tel. 646/183-9501, www.baronbalche.com, daily 10 A.M.–4 P.M.) is another boutique winery using the latest technology to make wine—10,000 cases a year.

The largest winery in the region—and in all of Latin America—Italian-owned **L. A. Cetto** (Km 73.5, tel. 646/155-2179, www.cettowines.com or www.lacetto.com, daily 10 A.M.–3 P.M.) has gardens and a picnic area, as well as an inviting tasting room. You can tour the winery without reservations, and there are no tasting or tour fees. Past L. A. Cetto, **La Casa de Doña Lupe** (Rancho La Gotita, Francisco Zarco, tel. 646/155-2323, www.donalupe.com, daily 9 A.M.–7 P.M.) tempts visitors with home-baked goods, as well as farm-fresh cheese, honey, and produce and organically grown wines. In the same vicinity, you'll pay US$2.50 to taste the tempranillo, graciano, and mazuelo varietals at **Casa Pedro Domecq** (Km 73.5, tel. 646/155-2333, www.vinosdomecq.com.mx, Mon.–Fri. 10 A.M.–4 P.M., Sat. 10 A.M.–5 P.M.). The fee includes a cellar tour, plus use of a picnic area on the grounds.

Also at Domecq, **GaleríAH** (Mexico 3, Km 73, tel. 646/175-3132, www.galeriah.com.mx) represents contemporary artists from Mexico around the world.

Baja Wine Country Tours

Local resident Steve Dryden (U.S. tel. 619/300-4976, www.mexicowinetours.com) offers wine-tasting tours by private van or motor coach. Day-long bus tours depart from San Diego and include tastings at three wineries and lunch at Mustafa's Moroccan Restaurant. Steve is a former Napa Valley winery manager with extensive knowledge of the Mexican wine industry, as well as the Kumiai people, Russian (Molokan) history, and the culture and history of Baja California. To follow the action in Baja's wine country, read his *Baja Times* column online (www.bajatimes.com/bajawine.asp).

Fiesta de la Vendimía Bajacaliforniana

Each August, the Valle de Guadalupe wineries celebrate a 10-day winemaking festival with tastings, food/wine pairings, vineyard tours, and the requisite music and dancing, in the valley and in downtown Ensenada. For information on upcoming festivals, call 646/174-0170 or Bodegas de Santo Tomás in Ensenada (tel. 646/178-3333) or contact CANIRAC, the Ensenada restaurant association (www.caniracensenada.com).

ACCOMMODATIONS AND CAMPING
Under US$50

Budget travelers can rent a cottage for US$35 a night at **Viños Sueños** (tel. 646/179-4763, daily 9 A.M.–5 P.M.) winery in Francisco Zarco.

US$50-100

Warm colors set the tone in affordable rooms at **El Mezon del Vino** (tel. 664/162-9010, www.elmezondelvino.com, US$60 weekdays, US$80 weekends, suites US$150). Book an in-room massage for US$45. The hotel has a restaurant (weekends 8 A.M.–7 P.M.) for wine-tasting as well as breakfast and lunch.

US$100-250

Tuscan-style **La Villa del Valle** (6 km. west of Mexico 3 from Km. 88 btw San Antonio de las Minas and Ejido El Porvenirtel. 646/183-9249, U.S. tel. 818/207-7130, www.lavilladelvalle.com, US$175) stands atop a hill on 28 hectares with sweeping views of surrounding vineyards, orchards, and gardens. Four of its six rooms have private balconies; all have luxury linens and many more elegant touches. In between tastings, guests relax by the pool or soak in the hot tub, book a massage on-site, or play a game of bocce ball. Rates include full breakfast, an afternoon glass of wine and *botanas*, and Wi-Fi access. There is a two-night minimum on weekends.

Near the Monte Xanic and Chateau Camou wineries, the **Adobe Guadalupe B&B** (Francisco Zarco, tel. 646/155-2094, www.adobeguadalupe.com, US$168) was the first winery to offer accommodations in the valley. The 24-hectare winery offers six guestrooms in a rambling adobe-walled, hacienda-style complex. Rates include a complete breakfast served at a common table in the huge kitchen. Other meals may be arranged per cost. In recent years, some guests have complained of overly protective dogs roaming common areas of the inn (reportedly, they do bite) and less-than-attentive service. Also note that double beds are twins pushed together.

Camping

You can camp on an 32-hectare farm at **Bibayoff-Bodegas Valle de Guadalupe** (tel. 646/177-2722, bibayoff@telnor.net), run by a Russian family in San Antonio de las Minas. Exit Mexico 3 at El Tigre and follow the dirt road to Rancho Bibayoff. The Kumiai have opened a campground just north of L. A. Cetto Winery. Some say it resembles a California state park at the turn of the 20th century. Sites cost US$5, and services include firewood, water, showers, and a general store. Guided hikes, horseback riding, cultural displays, and crafts are also available. Reservations are required. Contact Horacio Moncada at tel. 646/178-8093 or 646/118-9113.

FOOD

The valley now has a few well-known restaurants to go with its boutique wineries: Around 22 kilometers northeast of Ensenada, perched on a hill just north of the small community of San Antonio de las Minas, **Restaurant Mustafa** (Km 93, tel. 646/155-3185, Wed.–Mon. 8 A.M.–7 P.M., mains US$7–12) serves Moroccan-influenced dishes, including lamb shish-kebab and chicken breast stuffed with spinach and cheese, along with a menu of Mexican specialties. In San Antonio itself, **El Mesón** is popular for breakfast and lunch; it's closed on Thursday. The owner is an admirer of British aviation artist Robert Taylor and displays Taylor's work on the restaurant walls.

Visiting gourmands praise **Restaurant Laja** (Km 83, tel. 646/155-2556, www.lajamexico. com, prix fixe menu US$52 or US$72) for farm-fresh cuisine on par with California's celebrated Chez Panisse and French Laundry restaurants. The brainchild of former Four Seasons chef Jair Téllez, the restaurant is located about 50 meters off Mexico 3 via a washboard road, in a private home with white walls and a red tile roof.

In Francisco Zarco, **Doña Chuy's** (Km. 83 Mexico 3, Francisco Zarco, no tel., mains under US$10) has reasonably priced Mexican plates, and **La Cabaña de las Lomas** (Km 91.5, Cajeme St., tel. 646/155-3033, www.lacabanadelaslomas. com, Fri.–Sun. 8 A.M.–5 P.M.) prepares northern Mexican specialties such as fresh quail.

Mercado La Chica and **Abarrotes C. R.,** both in Francisco Zarco, can meet basic needs for food and supplies.

GETTING THERE

The Valle de Guadalupe is less than a two-hour drive (113 km) south of San Diego on the toll road from Tijuana to Ensenada. After paying the last toll, watch for a sign to Tecate via Mexico 3 and the Ruta del Vino. Travel east on Mexico 3 for 11 kilometers until you drop down into the Baja wine country at San Antonio de las Minas. This is the western end of the Guadalupe Valley wine region, which extends 22 kilometers east toward Tecate, ending near Km 73.5 at L. A. Cetto and Domecq wineries.

Sierra Juárez

The least-traveled highway on the Baja Peninsula, Mexico 3, connects Ensenada to Mexico 5 and San Felipe on the Sea of Cortez. Along the way, it passes a Dominican mission site, provides access to a small national park, Constitución de 1857, and crosses the Sierra Juárez via the San Matías Pass.

There are four places to buy gas along the route: Ojos Negros (Km 39), Independencia (Km 94), as well as Lázaro Cárdenas and

Francisco R. Serrano, closer to the east end of the highway.

PARQUE NACIONAL CONSTITUCIÓN DE 1857

This 5,000-hectare park covers a sub-alpine plateau in the center of the Sierra Juárez range. Granite boulders and Ponderosa pines ring its two natural lakes, Laguna La Chica and Laguna Juárez (Laguna Hanson). The latter has campsites (US$5) with fire pits and grills, but there are no marked hiking trails in the park.

The park is generally deserted except during Semana Santa (the week before Easter), when off-roaders invade. Be prepared for snow in winter.

Getting There

The easiest access road to the park heads northeast off Mexico 3 at Km 55 near Ojos Negros. This route is mostly paved now, and is passable for most vehicles, except after winter storms.

If you don't want to retrace your steps to Mexico 3, you can continue on the access road heading northeast to the other side of the park, and meet Mexico 2 60 kilometers from Laguna Hanson, near La Rumorosa.

MISIÓN SANTA CATALINA VIRGEN Y MÁRTIR

Padre José Loriente founded this mission (1797–1840) to the west of a strategic mountain pass that led to the San Felipe desert and the Colorado River beyond. At 1,067 meters, the mission was built to serve as a fort, protecting the coastal missions against raids from indigenous people to the east. At one time, it claimed the most converts of any Dominican mission on the peninsula, but it was destroyed in 1840 in a rebel attack. Only traces of the mission walls remain in the present-day village of Santa Catarina, which is eight kilometers east of Independencia (Km 94) along a graded dirt road.

Maneadero to Vicente Guerrero

Between Ensenada and San Quintín, Mexico 1 meanders inland along low mesas, through the fertile valley of Santo Tomás, and on south past a series of ranchos and agricultural supply towns. Four Dominican mission sites dot the highway along the way.

MANEADERO

Once you pass into the farming town of Maneadero, 20 kilometers south of Ensenada, you've reached the end of the "free zone" and will need immigration papers (tourist card or visa) to proceed farther south. The military often has a checkpoint set up here, and the *topes* (speed bumps) are plentiful, so take it slow.

Accommodations and Camping

Las Cañadas Campamento (Km 31–32, tel. 646/153-1055, toll-free U.S. tel. 800/027-3828, www.lascanadas.com, US$16 pp) originally opened as a day-use swimming complex in the summer, but it also has a few campsites with full hookups and lakeside tent camping, both of which are open year-round. Basic cabins rent for US$65 per night; bring your own linens.

LA BOCANA AND PUERTO SANTO TOMÁS

The first opportunity for off-road exploration south of Ensenada comes at Km 46–47, where a gravel road heads west, following the Cañon Santo Tomás to the coast. Sheltered by Punta Santo Tomás to the north, the fishing settlements of La Bocana and Puerto Santo Tomás have free camping on the beach and cabins for rent. *Panga* fishing and kayak fishing are popular activities, with rock cod and snapper among the common catches. There is a boat launch for small watercraft, and the kelp beds in the bay could make for an interesting dive if you have your own equipment.

There are a couple of *tiendas*, but don't count on much. You're off the grid here, so phones and other power-intensive amenities aren't going to be available. Cell phones don't get much of a signal either. It takes about an hour and a half to get to Puerto Santo Tomás by car.

Surfing

Surfers find occasional reef and point breaks in Bahía Santo Tomás and at Punta China to the south (turn left when you reach the coastal road and La Bocana). But the waves are more consistent and the rides often longer at the next point south, Punta San José. Popular with surfers from San Diego, the point has free cliffside camping above the surf, with outhouses but no services. There are two ways to reach San José. The best road leaves the highway just south of the Pemex in Santo Tomás. Go about 23 kilometers and bear right at the fork; continue another 16 kilometers to the lighthouse and camping area. Alternatively, if you have a high-clearance vehicle you might attempt an ungraded road that branches south from the Cañon Puerto Santo Tomás road, about 20.5 kilometers west of Mexico 1. From the turnoff, it's about 11 kilometers of rough driving to the break. Inquire in town about the road conditions before you choose this route.

Accommodations

The **Puerto Santo Tomás Resort** (Ensenada message tel. 646/154-9415, www.puertosantotomas.com, realbaja@starband.net) has rustic cabins (US$40–50) and larger houses (US$100–150) for rent, as well as campsites (US$14, includes showers and toilets) and a cantina serving Mexican and seafood dishes. You need to book ahead to eat here so the management can get the supplies it needs in time for your arrival. *Panga* fishing rates are US$130–160 per day. To find the resort, look for a road sign for Puerto Santo Tomás between Km 46–47 and turn right about 45 meters after the sign. (If you reach the village of Santo Tomás on Mexico 1, you've passed the turn.) Follow this road 29 kilometers west, staying right each time the road forks. The road meets the coast at La Bocana (The Mouth). Turn right (north) and follow the road over a small hill and along the coast for about five kilometers to Puerto Santo Tomás.

◖ VALLE DE SANTO TOMÁS

You know you've entered the agricultural valley of Santo Tomás (pop. 400) when you start to see rolling hills covered in a carpet of brilliant green, rows of grapevines, olive groves, and fields of wildflowers.

Misíon Santo Tomás de Aquino

Dominican Padre José Loriente established this mission (1791–1849) midway between Misíon San Miguel to the north and San Vicente to the south. He planted to raise livestock and planted the first mission crops, including olives and grapes. The mission's wine became known all over the peninsula, and the Bodegas de Santo Tomás continues the tradition today.

The mission had a prosperous but turbulent history. Indigenous people here were less receptive to missionary efforts than those the Jesuits had first encountered in Southern Baja, and two of the resident priests would be murdered before the mission was secularized in 1849.

There are two places to see what little remains of the mission ruins (a few adobe mounds, barely recognizable). The Dominicans built the original buildings west of Mexico 1, on a low mesa off the gravel road that parallels the Cañon Santo Tomás. Later, the community moved to the present-day village of Santo Tomás, east of the highway and north of the Palomar Trailer Park.

Bodegas de Santo Tomás

Founded in 1888, this winery (Rancho los Dolores, Mexico 1, Km 49, Ensenada office tel. 646/178-3333, daily 11 A.M.–3 P.M.) owns the majority of the vineyards in the Valle de Santo Tomás and also has an office in Ensenada. It makes a highly regarded wine called Duetto, through a partnership with Wente Vineyard of California. The winery offers group tours by reservation only.

Accommodations and Food

A mainstay on the Northern Baja travel circuit for more than half a century, **El Palomar** (Mexico 1, Km 51–52, Santo Tomás, tel. 646/153-8002, www.elpalomar.ws, edgaryarce@hotmail.com) consists of a restaurant (daily 7 A.M.–10 P.M., mains start at US$7), motel (US$18 pp), campground with two swimming pools, and Pemex station. The campsites and pool are in an olive grove on the east side of the highway (and you have to descend a steep driveway to get there), but the office, restaurant, motel, and Pemex are on the west side at the base of a hill as you come around a bend in the road. RV camping costs US$16.50 per night for two people (full hook-ups) and includes two free margaritas.

ERÉNDIRA AND PUERTO SAN ISIDRO

For another side trip to the coast, turn west from Mexico 1 at Km 78 on the paved road that leads out to the Ejido Eréndira. There is a sign for Coyote Cal's at the turn. The road winds 24 kilometers through a canyon to the nondescript village of Eréndira (pop. 1,500). Head north along the dirt road five kilometers to Coyote Cal's hostel, at the end of the power lines.

Three more kilometers north along the coast will bring you to Punta Cabras. South of this point, Half Moon Bay is protected from the prevailing northwest winds and catches the summertime south swells. Long Beach, to the north of the point, catches most swells and offers plenty of peaks, unless the onshore winds are killing it. There have been numerous reports of thefts in the area around River's Mouth, but you can leave valuables at Coyote Cal's for safekeeping.

Fishing

About 1.5 kilometers north of Eréndira, you'll find San Isidro Cove. The buildings on the cliff on the north side above the boat ramp are **Castro's Place** (tel. 646/176-2897). Vicente Castro starting fishing the area in 1949, and now his kids run the operation. They use a rusty tractor to tow their *pangas* in and out of the cove. With experienced captains, the bottom fishing in this area is a no-brainer and a *panga*-load of four anglers can fill a 100-quart cooler in a day. Surface fishing for yellowtail and dorado is possible, but the best opportunities are on the bottom. Castro's provides bait, licenses, and gear, but you can use your own if you prefer. There are also clean cabins with bunks for US$25–30 per night, and you can camp for a nominal fee.

Accommodations

Coyote Cal's Mexico Hostels (Ejido Eréndira, tel. 646/154-4080, www.coyotecals. com) is turning into a classic Baja meeting place for surfers, European backpackers, and touring motorcyclists. One of the reasons for its popularity is that there is a room for every budget. You can camp out front on the "beach" (a sandy front yard) for US$10, plus US$3 for breakfast (mid-sized RVs okay if self-contained). On the other end of the spectrum, there's the top-floor Crow's Nest room for US$60 per night (three-night minimum, reserve online) with panoramic views of the surrounding cliffs and ocean. Bunks go for a reasonable US$15–18 per person and private rooms are US$45–50 per couple. The hostel also rents surfboards, mountain bikes, and snorkeling gear. Its new Barefoot Cantina serves XX lager, Sol, and Tecate beer, as well as a menu of mixed drinks. The cantina does not serve meals, however, so plan to buy your own supplies in Ensenada on the way down.

Getting There

Many budget travelers reach Coyote Cal's without their own transportation. Bus fare from Ensenada costs about US$11 and drops you off at Km 78. From here, you need to hitch a ride (easy to do, according to those who've done it). Catch the bus before 2 P.M. to reach the hostel before dark. Alternatively, stay on the bus until San Vicente. When you depart, look across the street and to the left of the Pemex for Mimi Hotel. Inquire here about taxi service (tel. 646/165-6747, available 24/7 for US$25–30) to the hostel. You'll need to speak Spanish to arrange the ride.

A third option is to hire a station wagon taxi from Ensenada (US$75 flat fee, negotiate before you get in and tell the driver the trip will include about five kilometers of dirt road driving, to avoid extra costs). The taxi can stop at the Calimax store, where you can buy food, and then bring you directly to the hostel.

SAN VICENTE

The next valley south of Santo Tomás is almost as picturesque, with more agricultural crops and the Llano Colorado (Reddish Plain) beyond it. The town itself (pop. 3,500) is a small-sized commercial center, with a few restaurants and stores, as well as an ABC bus terminal—all right along the highway. The only real point of interest here is the historic Dominican mission of San Vicente Ferrer, located one kilometer north of town, at Km 88.

Misión San Vicente Ferrer
Founded by Padres Miguel Hidalgo and Joaquín Valero in 1780, this mission (1780–1833) and military outpost played an important role in connecting the Baja California missions to the newer settlements in Alta California. It also had one of the largest building complexes of any Dominican mission. In 1997, Mexico's Instituto Nacional de Antropología e Historia (INAH) began an archeological dig to uncover, reinforce, and protect the remaining mission ruins. Today, the site is lined with gravel paths and the adobe walls are covered in a waterproof layer. To find the mission site, look for a dirt road heading west off Mexico 1, just south of Km 88.

COLONET AND SAN ANTONIO DEL MAR
The farming town of Colonet has a Pemex and handful of places to eat and shop. Use it as a supply station for trips to the coast or into the sierra. There aren't any sights of interest in the town proper.

Almost due west of Colonet, San Antonio del Mar is a remote beach camp on an estuary with a few homes and trailers. The exposed, sandy beach faces west, and there are good shore fishing and decent beachbreaks in both directions. This is a good bet to escape the crowds. Stock up on supplies and fill your tank with gas in Colonet. Primitive camping with no facilities costs US$5 per night. Turn off Mexico 1 at Km 126, a little north of town and just before the bridge. From here, it's 12.5 kilometers to the coast.

Bahía Colonet (14 km southwest) is supposedly a target for development as part of the Escalera Nautica project, but nothing has materialized to date. The north point of this bay, Cabo Colonet, breaks on northwest swells. On the bay itself, **Cuatro Casas** is one of the more crowded longboarding breaks along this stretch of coastline. It is also a fickle spot that doesn't break consistently.

Crime warning: An armed robbery of a surf instructor and longtime Baja traveler was widely reported in the San Diego press in 2007. He was camping with his girlfriend in a deserted spot along the coast after getting lost on the road to Cuatro Casas after dark. Take precautions when exploring this area. Leave your valuables behind, travel in groups, camp at the hostel, and don't be conspicuous.

Accommodations and Camping
On an exposed bluff overlooking the break, **Cuatro Casas Hostel Surf** (U.S. tel. 619/756-0639, www.myspace.com/cuatrocasas) has a variety of clean rooms starting at US$15 in a large house, and camping for US$5. The parking area is fenced, and the owner has a bright spotlight on the roof to ward off would-be intruders. In recent years, we've seen short-sighted fishermen out front using bleach to ferret out octopuses from their holes in the tidepools.

To find Cuatro Casas coming from the north on Mexico 1, drive 13.8 kilometers south of Colonet to a Pemex on the left and then another kilometer and a half on the highway after that toward the intersection with the paved road to San Telmo. After you pass a yellow auto parts store, turn right onto a dirt road that leads to the coast (12.9 km). Call or text the owner, Richard, for reservations.

PUNTA SAN JACINTO
Nine kilometers west of Camalú on Mexico 1 via a wide, graded dirt road, Punta San Jacinto offers surfing and primitive camping on a sandy but exposed beach. The turnoff to Punta San Jacinto comes between Km 149–150 on Mexico 1.

The town of Camalú, beginning at Km 157, can meet most basic traveler needs with its several markets, pharmacies, and eateries. There is also an auto mechanic and Pemex station with diesel fuel. Directly west of town (turn right at the stoplight north of the Pemex and drive straight out to the beach), Punta Camalú is a worthwhile right point break, reportedly more consistent than Cuatro Casas to the north.

Surfing
The surf is found at the site of a huge freighter, *Isla del Carmen,* that is beached on the sand. It's a soft wave, but a good choice for days when the northwest swell is huge. **Baja Surf Adventures** (toll-free U.S. tel. 800/428-7873, www.bajasurfadventures.com, baja.bill@gmail.com) runs a solar-powered resort here providing lessons and basic accommodations for up to 16 guests.

Camping
You can camp for free on the sand dunes behind the beach, but it's not recommended since crime in this area is a real concern.

VICENTE GUERRERO
As a regional hub for agricultural commerce, Colonia Vicente Guerrero (pop. 10,600) has a post office, police station, and medical clinic, as well as a grocery store, ATMs, and several places to eat. The Pemex is open around the clock. ABC buses stop here, and there are three RV parks in town.

Migrant workers from mainland Mexico tend to crops of tomatoes and strawberries in the surrounding fields. On the coast, surf-casting is a popular pastime for locals and visitors alike.

Misión Santo Domingo de la Frontera
Padres Miguel Hidalgo and Manuel García founded the second Dominican mission (1775–1839) in Baja near the Arroyo Santo Domingo, northeast of Vicente Guerrero. Although it occupied a strategic location, with ample freshwater and easy coastal access, the mission grew slowly at first. It produced large quantities of corn and wheat and traded otter furs with ships that came to nearby San Quintín. But the indigenous people suffered from disease, and the mission was abandoned in 1839.

During its life, the mission occupied three sites in the Vicente Guerrero area. Ruins at the third and final site are among the most recognizable of all the ruins on the peninsula. Mexico's INAH agency has protected the site by reinforcing the crumbling adobe walls, putting a fence around the mission quadrangle, and adding an entry kiosk. A building on-site now contains a small collection of items from the mission era.

Accommodations and Camping
RV caravans often spend the night at **Posada Don Diego RV Park and Restaurant** (off Mexico 1 at Km 174, tel. 616/166-2181, www.posadadondiego.com, posadadondiego@yahoo.com, daily 8 A.M.–9 P.M.). Under its current ownership since 1979, this park has 100 campsites (50 with full hookups for US$11, the rest with electricity and water only for US$10), plus four motel-style rooms for US$35. There are also a three-bedroom house and four trailers for rent. On-site activities include basketball and volleyball. Its restaurant serves Mexican plates, a full lineup of steaks, baby back ribs, and seafood dishes, all at reasonable prices. Breakfast mains cost US$3.50–9 and dinners are US$7–14.

To find Posada Don Diego, go about a kilometer and a half south of the only stoplight in town Vicente Guerrero and turn right (west) just before the propane plant.

Sierra de San Pedro Mártir

For true wilderness seekers, the highest mountain range on the Baja Peninsula offers a dramatic change from the desert and coastal scenery below. Lodgepole pines, quaking aspens, and the endemic San Pedro Mártir cypress are just a few of the unusual trees that have attached themselves to the slopes and canyons of the Sierra de San Pedro Mártir. The rare *borregón* (bighorn sheep) lives in the range, and the California condor was recently reintroduced.

At 3,095 meters, the tallest peak in the range, Picacho del Diablo (Devil's Peak), also goes by the names Cerro de la Encantada (Enchanted Mountain) and La Providencia (Providence). Its two granite peaks are often capped with snow in winter. Experienced backpackers typically approach the summit from the eastern side in a three-day trip.

◪ PARQUE NACIONAL SIERRA SAN PEDRO MÁRTIR

Founded by a presidential decree in 1974, this 68,796-hectare national park centers around the San Pedro Mártir Plateau (elevation 1,800 m), which covers approximately 70 kilometers by 15 kilometers at the north end of the range. Given its remote location, it is one of the least visited national parks in all of Mexico, which can make a trip here all the more enjoyable.

The park entrance is located 78 kilometers from Mexico 1 via a paved road that heads west from Mexico 1 at San Telmo; follow signs marked Observatorio. The park is open daily 7 A.M.–7 P.M., and the entry fee is US$7.50 per vehicle. Another way to access the Sierra de San Pedro Mártir is via a rough dirt road (high clearance required) through the farming town of Valle de la Trinidad, off Mexico 3 (Km 121). This route is 48-kilometers long and takes you to the northern boundary of the national park.

OBSERVATORIO ASTRONÓMICO NACIONAL

Clear air and nonexistent light pollution led the Mexican government to choose Cerro de la Cúpula (elevation 2,830 m) as the location for a

ENSENADA TO EL ROSARIO

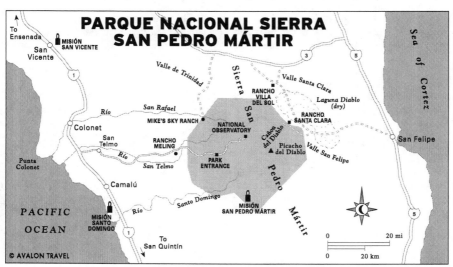

PARQUE NACIONAL SIERRA SAN PEDRO MÁRTIR

© AVALON TRAVEL

MAJOR BAJA CALIFORNIA MOUNTAIN RANGES

Range	Highest Peak	Summit Elevation
Sierra de San Pedro Mártir	Picacho del Diablo	3,095 meters (10,154 ft)
Sierra de la Laguna	Picacho de la Laguna	2,161 meters (7,090 ft)
Sierra de San Francisco	Pico Santa Monica	2,104 meters (6,904 ft)
Sierra San Borja	Pico Echeverría	1,907 meters (6,258 ft)
Sierra Juárez	Cerro Torre Blanco	1,800 meters (5,904 ft)
Sierra de la Giganta	Cerro La Giganta	1,765 meters (5,792 ft)
Sierra de la Asamblea	Cerro Dos Picachos	1,658 meters (5,438 ft)
Sierra de Guadalupe	Monte Thetis	1,640 meters (5,380 ft)

world-class observatory, called the Observatorio Astronómico Nacional (Ensenada tel. 646/174-4580, www.astrosen.unam.mx, contacto@ astrosen.unam.mx, Sat. 11 A.M.–1 P.M., by reservation). Built in 1975, its three telescopes (2.1 meters, 1.5 meters, and 84 centimeters) assess the brightness of the sky, the state of the atmosphere, and a long list of meteorological data. This facility is regarded as one of the best places on the planet to observe the stars and planets above. It's open to the public, but hours are limited and vary by the season.

The observatory is located at the end of the park access road, also called the San Telmo de Abajo road (20 km past the park entrance). Park before the locked gate and walk the final two kilometers to the buildings.

MISIÓN SAN PEDRO MÁRTIR DE VERONA

Dominican Padre José Loriente established a mountain mission (1794–1824) high in the Sierra San Pedro Mártir to serve a small population of indigenous people, but the rugged terrain and cold winter climate made for a challenging mission environment. Its 20-hectare orchard grew wheat, corn, and beans primarily. Only the faint ruins of a few walls survive

today, and access is difficult: from the observatory, it's a two-day guided horseback ride to reach the site.

HIKING AND CAMPING

Backcountry hikes and self-contained camping are permitted within the park, but infrastructure and services are limited. Few trails are marked, so you'll need to bring a GPS and topo maps (*San Rafael H11B45* and *Santa Cruz H11B55*), which Santa Barbara, California–based **Mexico Maps** (U.S. tel. 805/687-1011, www.mexicomaps.com) sells for US$15.95 per map. The easiest trails to follow are located along the northeastern edge of the park, near the observatory. If you're not confident that you can navigate the wilderness environment on your own, you can hire a guide through Meling Ranch (tel. 646/179-4106, www.melingguestranch.com) or EcoTur (www.mexonline.com/baja/ecotur3.htm).

Hunting and the possession of firearms (even with a Mexican permit) are prohibited, as is off-road driving. You can build campfires in fire rings at a few sites in the park. As with any wilderness environment, let the local rangers know the details of your trip before you head off on the trail.

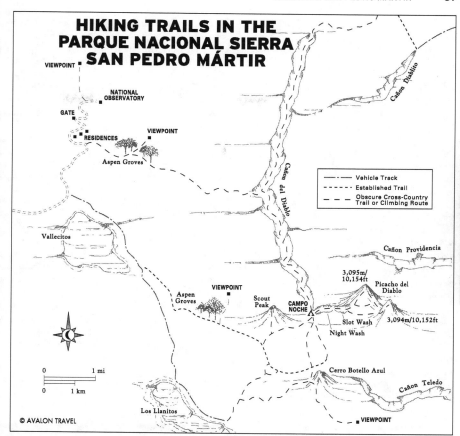

HIKING TRAILS IN THE PARQUE NACIONAL SIERRA SAN PEDRO MÁRTIR

Summer temps hover around 26°C during the day, dropping to 4.5°C at night. July and August also bring heavy rains and afternoon thunderstorms to the sierra. In winter, temperatures range 4.5°C to 12°C, and snowfall is common above 2,000 meters. Days are pleasantly warm in spring and fall, but night can dip below freezing.

Accordingly, the best hiking seasons are mid-April–mid-June, when the wildflowers are in bloom and fresh water is plentiful, and late September–early November, before the snows begin.

ACCOMMODATIONS
Rancho Meling

Between Km 140–141, a newly paved road goes east to the settlement of San Telmo and then climbs into the Sierra San Pedro Mártir. Along the way, 50 kilometers from the highway, the historic Rancho Meling has been entertaining and feeding adventurous guests since the turn of the 20th century.

Owned and operated by the Johnson/ Meling families since 1910, Rancho Meling (also known as Rancho San José, tel. 646/179-4106, www.melingguestranch.com, US$50 pp) was born as a base for gold-mining operations and then destroyed by bandits in the Mexican Revolution. It was rebuilt as a 4,000-hectare cattle ranch, and today, it is a haven for motorcyclists, eco-tourists, fly-in guests, and anyone seeking the solitude of a rustic getaway in the mountains.

The working cattle ranch sits at an elevation of 670 meters in a stand of pines at the base of the sierra. Its 12 rooms all have private baths, hot water, and a fireplace or wood stove for heat. For larger groups or families, there is a four-bedroom/three-bath cabin. Hearty meals (breakfast/lunch/dinner US$6/8/11) are cooked over a wood-fired stove and served at a long wooden table beside a large stone fireplace in the main house. The generator goes off at 10 P.M., but you can read by the light of a kerosene lamp after that.

The road to San Telmo comes 13.9 kilometers south of Colonet, just past a Pemex on the left. (Fill up before you head into the sierra.) Alternatively, you can fly your own plane and land on the ranch's dirt landing strip. Baja Bush Pilots members receive 10 percent off daily rates.

Mike's Sky Ranch

Just beyond Km 138 on Mexico 3, a dirt road heads 35.5 kilometers south to Mike's Sky Ranch (tel. 664/681-5514), a rustic resort in the sierra foothills (elevation 1,200 m) at the northwestern edge of the national park. Popular with off-road bikers, the ranch has been a checkpoint on the Baja 500 and Baja 1000 races for many years. Accommodations are in 27 basic cabins (US$60 pp), and the rates include family-style meals and use of the swimming pool. Campsites cost US$5 per vehicle per night (water and shower use only). Campers can pay US$12 additional for dinner and US$7 for breakfast (served 6–10 A.M. and lunch.

The road to Mike's is rough in spots and can change drastically with recent rains. Beyond the ranch, this road continues southwestward to join the newly paved road between Mexico 1 and the national park.

GETTING AROUND
Guided Trips

Ensenada native Francisco Detrell has been organizing sierra tours since the 1980s through his company **EcoTur** (Blvd. Costero #1094, Local 14, Ensenada, www.mexonline.com/baja/ecotur3.htm, ecoturbc@ens.com.mx, tours US$12–150). Guided trips include waterfall hikes, Picacho del Diablo summits, and observatory tours. Francisco speaks English and Spanish.

Meling Ranch also offers guided hikes into the sierra.

Valle and Bahía de San Quintín

South of Vicente Guerrero on Mexico 1, the wide, flat coastal plain of San Quintín begins. Two rivers, Río San Miguel and Río Santa María, provide water that fuels the local agricultural economy. Workers' camps on the outskirts of town house farm workers from mainland Mexico, who come to work the fields.

Visitors who stopover here—mainly the sportfishing set—enjoy a unique coastal environment that consists of three connected bays: narrow Bahía San Quintín and Bahía Falsa, and the larger Bahía Santa María. In between are tidal zones and marshes filled with marine life.

The town of San Quintín itself (pop. 20,000) offers some practical services for travelers (clinic, banks, Internet), but is primarily another agricultural hub. Five kilometers south of San Quintín, Lázaro Cárdenas, has Mexico's 67th Infantry battalion camp, an intercity bus terminal, and some shops and restaurants.

HISTORY

Named by Sebastián Vizcaíno, San Quintín caught the attention of foreign investors as early as the 1880s as a potentially lucrative

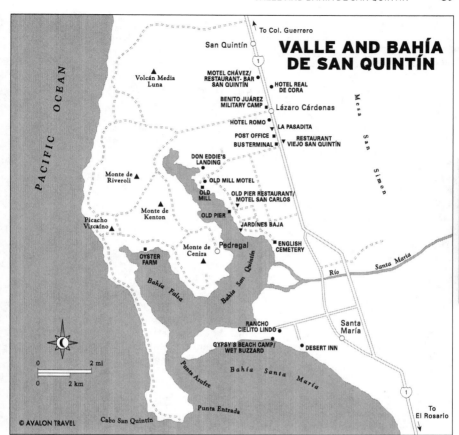

VALLE AND BAHÍA DE SAN QUINTÍN

wheat-growing area; however, early colonists, first from the United States and later from England, failed to realize the vision. Before giving up, they dredged the harbor, dug wells, laid train tracks, and set up gristmill machinery—the remains of which you can still see along the inner bay shoreline today.

In the 1950s and '60s, San Quintín captured the imagination of some pioneering anglers from the United States, and the first few resorts opened for business. Among them, the Old Mill Motel became a legend in its time.

Today, a small community of expats lives on the bayfront in a neighborhood called Pedregal, and a few fishing lodges cater to the sportfishing crowd.

SPORTS AND RECREATION
Beach and Bay Access

Follow signs to the Old Mill Motel from Mexico 1 to reac h the bay. You can launch small boats here or from the Pedregal area on the west shore of the bay. Follow a gravel road from Mexico 1 (btw the Pemex and military camp) west of Lázaro Cárdenas 14 kilometers to Bahía Falsa. When the road forks, take the left (south) branch to reach Pedregal.

Alternatively, continue west at the fork another few hundred meters to Ostiones Guerrero, where you may be able to buy fresh oysters by the dozen. The road ends at a fish camp on the ocean.

To reach Bahía Santa María, drive 16 kilometers south of Lázaro Cárdenas and turn right (west) on the paved road to Santa María. Follow signs to the Desert Inn Hotel; local clam diggers frequent Playa Santa María at low tide. It's a long, sandy beach, located just past the hotel.

Fishing and Hunting

The unique marine environment here, with the shallow bay system and several rocky seamounts just offshore in the Pacific, creates fantastic opportunities for both surf casting and deep sea fishing. Rock cod, yellowtail, and lingcod are common, and that's just the beginning of the list. Experienced anglers say they are able to catch upwards of 20 different species in one day of fishing.

The presence of several large-scale oyster farms along the inner bays shows just how clean the marine environment is. (They need pristine conditions to thrive.)

San Quintín Sportfishing (Rancho Cielito Lindo, tel. 616/165-6046, book4fish@aol.com), **Pedro's Pangas** (tel. 888/568-2252, www.pedrospangas.com), **Tiburon's Pangas Sportfishing** (near the Old Mill, U.S. tel. 619/428-2779), **Don Eddie's Landing** (tel. 616/165-6061), and **Campo Lorenzo** (tel. 616/165-6022 or Skype tel. 909/581-4140) can arrange guided fishing trips for around US$200–300 per *panga,* depending on the season.

San Quintín offers hunters the opportunity to pursue ducks and valley quail, but it's best known for the brandt hunting. Contact Lorenzo at Campo Lorenzo to arrange quail hunting. **Sporting Field International** (www.sportingfield.com) brokers pricey brandt hunts using local guides. The cost will end up being US$2,000 or so for a three-day hunt (Thursday–Sunday only). The season for brandt is January and Feburary.

Surfing

The beachbreaks along Playa San Ramón, which runs between Vicente Guerrero and San Quintín (access at Km 172), are nothing special, but they don't get crowded either. The better-known, but still uncrowded breaks are at Cabo San Quintín, with more consistent surf and longer rides. Access is difficult, via the road to Bahía Falsa and then a coastal road heading south to the point. Conditions are typically cold and super windy.

ACCOMMODATIONS AND CAMPING
Under US$50

Motel Chávez (San Quintín, tel. 616/165-2005, motelchavez@hotmail.com, US$20–30), next to a highway bridge toward the south end of town, has been a mainstay on the budget travel circuit for years. Its clean rooms have fans; cash only. Also on the highway, the **Hotel Real de Cora** (San Quintín, tel. 616/166-8576, US$32) has secure parking.

A relatively new option in town is the **Villa de San Quintín** (Av. A #5 btw 8th/9th, San Quintín, tel. 616/165-1800, www.hotellavilla.biz, US$35), an offshoot of a Tijuana hotel that was built in 2005. It has 32 non-smoking, carpeted rooms with private baths, and air-conditioning, TV, phone, and free high-speed Internet. Secure parking is designed for trailers and boats, and an on-site restaurant is open daily 6:30 A.M.–9:30 P.M.

At the northeast end of Bahía San Quintín, **Don Eddie's Landing** (tel. 616/165-6061, www.doneddies.com, US$45) has older rooms with lots of beds and sagging mattresses. Fishing packages are available and include lodging, boat, and food.

South of Don Eddie's Landing and next to the public boat launch, the **Old Mill Motel** (tel. 800/208-2154, U.S. tel. 619/428-2779, US$40–50) occupies the former gristmill site. A regular crowd of hunters and anglers frequents the place and they like to party at night. Accommodations are in cabins arranged around a courtyard, with an attached campground (US$10). Rates often include two

Rancho Cielito Lindo

cold beers. No heat or air-conditioning. The road out to these two places can get extremely muddy after a heavy rain; high clearance is recommended.

Next to Bahía Santa María, **Rancho Cielito Lindo** (U.S. tel. 619/593-2252, cielitolindo@ bajasi.com, US$10) is a restaurant and bar with a few rooms and a campground on the premises.

US$50-100

On Bahía Santa María, the **Desert Inn** (tel. 616/165-9008, toll-free U.S. tel. 800/800-9632, www.desertinns.com/sanquintin, US$75) was remodeled in 2004 in cool blue tones with floral spreads and drapes. Spacious rooms have remote-control heat and air-conditioning units, plus sea views and terraces. Modern tiled baths have glass shower doors; full-size bath towels are a treat. A palm-lined walkway leads to the beach. If you find yourself in the area at sundown and you don't want to shack up in a sportfishing lodge, this hotel is a good bet for a quiet night's sleep.

The newly renovated **C Hotel Jardines Baja** (U.S. tel. 619/591-8922, www.hotel-jardinesbaja.com, US$50–75) has raised the bar considerably for accommodations in the San Quintín area. It has several rooms, including a suite with its own deck and separate living room; some of the rooms have working wood-burning fireplaces. Its new restaurant opened in 2008 to rave reviews. Beds are comfortable, the grounds are beautiful, and the coffee is strong. Those who have discovered it are hoping the word doesn't get out too soon. Watch for the Jardines sign on Mexico 1, south of Lázaro Cárdenas, at the sign that points the way to Bahía San Quintín. Turn right and follow this road for about 1.5 kilometers to the sign for Hotel Baja Jardines. Turn left here and the hotel will be a few hundred meters down on the right.

Camping and RV Parks

One of the newcomers on the San Quintín scene for RV camping is **Los Olivos Family Park** (tel. 616/165-6123, US$15), popular because it is close to the highway, so you don't have to drive your big rig down a long bumpy dirt road just to crash for the night. This secure park has full hookups and a swimming pool, and hot showers were under construction at press time. It is located on the road to the Jardines Hotel and Restaurant.

If you prefer a beachside location, several places have been in business for decades: **Gypsy's Beach Camp** (no tel.) offers sites in a dirt lot for tent or RV camping for US$10 per night. Features include clean bathrooms, a two-story restaurant, and a dump station. A night watchman patrols the area 9 P.M.–5 A.M. **Rancho Cielito Lindo** (U.S. tel. 619/593-2252, cielitolindo@bajasi.com, RV/tent US$12/10) has 15 campsites—some with *palapas*—for tents or RVs.

A favorite among repeat Baja campers, **El Pabellón RV Campground** (Mexico 1, Km 16, US$5–10) is comfortably removed from the towns of San Quintín and Lázaro Cárdenas and set back from the highway. It has campsites in a large open lot fronting the beach, with water and sewer hookups, but no electricity. Restrooms are clean and have hot water. A fellow camper here once shared a delicious Peruvian-style ceviche, made of Pismo clams dug that day at the beach.

Beach camping is permitted but not recommended in the San Quintín area due to a persistent problem with theft.

FOOD

Take your pick of taco and *mariscos* stands that line the highway in both Lázaro Cárdenas and San Quintín. Clam cocktails are a local treat. **La Pasadita** (no tel., 9 A.M.–4 P.M., mains US$5) does reliable *tacos de pescado* on the plaza in Lázaro Cárdenas.

Pollos Lalos (daily 10 A.M.–10 P.M., US$5–10), on the west side of the highway in San Quintín, makes tasty *pollos al carbon*. Nearby **Tuco's Pizza** (daily 3–10 P.M., mains US$10) will satisfy your pizza cravings.

The best Mexican dining experience in the area awaits at **Restaurant Viejo San Quintín,** open daily for breakfast, lunch, and dinner (US$5–10). This friendly establishment is located between two pharmacies and across

from the post office in Lázaro Cárdenas. Order the *machaca,* chiles rellenos, carne asada, or enchiladas, and your beer will arrive in a frosted mug.

Gaston's Cannery (daily 5:30 A.M.–9:30 P.M., mains US$10–28) is part of the Old Mill complex. It serves Mexican food and seafood dinners, at relatively high prices for the area. If you're driving to the Old Mill Motel in the afternoon, make sure to pay attention to each turn along the way so you can find your way back when you drive back that evening. It's easy to get lost in the maze of sandy roads at night.

The **Hotel Jardines Baja** (U.S. tel. 619/591-8922, www.hotel-jardinesbaja.com, Tues.–Thurs. 8 A.M.–10 P.M., Fri.–Sun. 8 A.M.–2 A.M., mains US$10–15) opened its new restaurant in 2008 with a menu that features seafood, wings, and desserts.

Rancho Cielito Lindo (tel. 616/165-6046, U.S. reservations 619/593-2252, cielitolindo@bajasi.com, mains US$10) serves fresh seafood dishes at good prices (dinner only). Next door, **Wet Buzzard** (Gypsy's Beach Camp, no tel., tacos US$1 each) is known for its filling breakfasts. It also serves tacos and burritos for lunch.

Both San Quintín and Lázaro Cárdenas have *abarrotes* stores if you need to replenish food supplies.

INFORMATION AND SERVICES

There is a state tourism office between Vicente Guerrero and San Quintín at Km 178 on the west side of the highway. The office is officially open weekdays 8 A.M.–5 P.M., and weekends 10 A.M.–3 P.M., but hours tend to change with the seasons.

For medical emergencies, go to Clínica Santa María (tel. 616/165-2653, open 24 hours) in San Quintín.

GETTING THERE

San Quintín and Lázaro Cárdenas each have a Pemex station. There is an intercity bus depot in Lázaro Cárdenas, on the west side of Mexico 1; however, this area is not ideal for travelers without their own transportation, as the beaches are far from the highway.

Campo Lorenzo has a 760-meter unpaved licensed airstrip, air park, and trailer park for permanent residents. It is a private airstrip, but available to pilots who call ahead to Skype 909/581-4140 or the Mexican landline at 616/165-6022. The camp can make arrangements for transportation, and there is only a US$25 fee to land and park if you are staying at Don Eddie's.

El Rosario

Baja road-trippers tend to remember their first time passing through the commercial center of El Rosario (pop. 3,500) because it's the last chance to gas up before the long haul across the desert. As if to emphasize the point, the town has one of the largest Pemex stations in the area and it's open 24/7. There are two other reasons to hang around a while: If it's late in the day and you need a place to crash for the night, the Baja Cactus Motel has great rooms at unbelievably low prices. And if you just need a bite to eat on your way through, recently remodeled Ed's Baja's Best is a good bet.

MISÍON NUESTRA SEÑORA DEL ROSARIO DE VIÑADACO

The Dominicans established Misíon Nuestra Señora del Rosario De Viñadaco (1774–1832), the first of their nine Baja California missions, in present day El Rosario in 1774, led by Padres Vicente Mora and Francisco Galisteo. Adobe ruins of its second site are visible just off the west side of the highway at the sharp bend in the road. (Turn right at the grocery store and then left at the first road. Cross the arroyo and look for the ruins on the right.)

The standard mission crops of barley, corn, and beans grew especially well here, and the mission was able to convert hundreds of indigenous people before European illnesses began to take their toll on the population. By 1832, the mission was turned over to the local people.

ACCOMMODATIONS AND FOOD

Between the Pemex station and Mama Espinosa's restaurant, the **Baja Cactus Motel** (Km 55,

tel. 616/165-8850, www.bajacactus.com) has caused quite a stir among Transpeninsular insiders in recent years. Where else in the world can you enjoy all the amenities of a four-star establishment—immaculate tiled baths, granite counters, four-poster king-size beds, luxury linens, gorgeous woodwork, 29-inch satellite TVs, purified water, air conditioning—for US$35 a night? The story goes that the son of the motel owners wanted to help his parents fix the place up. All 22 rooms are wired with Ethernet cables, so that when high-speed Internet comes to El Rosario, Baja Cactus patrons will be among the first to enjoy it. You probably won't escape the sound of trucks decelerating through town, but you'll enjoy some of the finest accommodations anywhere on the peninsula.

The dining experience at historic **Mama Espinosa's** (east side of Mexico 1, just past the large Pemex as you enter the town from the north, no tel., daily breakfast, lunch, and dinner) has slipped of late, with higher prices (US$13–20) and disappointing meals. Stop in if you want to see all of the Baja 1000 memorabilia and learn a bit about the town's matriarch, Doña Anita, but lower your expectations for a memorable meal.

On the south side of town, recently remodeled **Baja's Best Café** (no tel., daily 7 A.M.–7 P.M., mains US$7–15) serves a mean breakfast with real sausage and dependable coffee. It also runs a bed-and-breakfast on the premises. Rooms have comfortable beds and rain showers (US$50).

El Rosario has several grocery stores that carry produce, bread, and basic household supplies. **Mercado Hermanos Jaramillo,** near Mama Espinosa's, is the best of the bunch.

MEXICALI TO SAN FELIPE

Among Baja's international border towns, agricultural Mexicali strikes a balance between bustling Tijuana and quiet Tecate. Its palm-lined boulevards are cleaner and less touristy than other Baja California cities of its size (pop. 1 million). In addition to farming, state government drives much of the local economy, as Mexicali is the capital of Baja California (Norte).

Across the border from Mexicali, smaller Calexico is in every way a symbiotic community—equally dependent on agriculture and related businesses. The whimsical names of the Mexicali and Calexico border towns reflect the laid-back tone in these sister cities. Outside of the immediate border-crossing area, the focus on tourism that colors the visitor's experience in Tijuana and Ensenada is largely absent. Among other Baja cities, Mexicali is most similar to La Paz in its mixed population of mainland Mexicans and foreign immigrants and the presence of a thriving local middle class. The city welcomes visitors, but its businesses do not cater to their every need. If you've had your fill of Americanized beach resorts with their activity booths and timeshare reps, Mexicali offers independent travelers a refreshing view of life in an ordinary Mexican city.

For California and Arizona residents, Mexicali is a gateway to both the Baja Peninsula and mainland Mexico. San Felipe and the northern beaches along the Sea of Cortez are just a couple of hours away by car. Southwest of Mexicali are plenty of opportunities for desert hiking, soaking in natural hot springs, and off-road racing, as well as some of the best fishing and hunting in the country.

HIGHLIGHTS

La Chinesca: Born of a lack of essential ingredients, Mexicali-style Chinese food has become a fusion cuisine all its own. Try it here, in the only true Chinatown in all of Mexico (page 80).

Cañon de Guadalupe: Hot springs in the Sierra Juárez above the San Felipe desert reward backcountry explorers willing to drive the washboard access road (page 87).

San Felipe *Malecón*: At night, the action in San Felipe takes place in discos and clubs along the waterfront. Start the evening off right with a seafood dinner in one of the town's open-air restaurants (page 90).

Valle de los Gigantes: Between San Felipe and Puertecitos, the Valle de los Gigantes is an ideal place to snap postcard-perfect images of the world's tallest cactus species, some of which live to be hundreds of years old (page 96).

Bahía San Luis Gonzaga: Popular with pilots and seasoned Baja travelers, this remote, gray-sand beach on the Gulf coast offers a slice of the old Baja (page 98).

LOOK FOR ❰ TO FIND RECOMMENDED SIGHTS, ACTIVITIES, DINING, AND LODGING.

PLANNING YOUR TIME

It takes about two hours to drive to Mexicali from the San Diego airport. Once you've arrived, you could spend just an afternoon and evening getting oriented and preparing for a trip to San Felipe, or a couple of days to explore the city's few attractions.

The most popular weekend itinerary in this area is a trip from Mexicali to San Felipe and back (two hours by car each way).

With a week or more, you could add a side trip to the Cañon de Guadalupe, and continue south of San Felipe to Puertecitos. With a four-wheel-drive vehicle, you could turn this trip into a loop, following the coastal road all the way to Gonzaga Bay and heading inland to meet the Transpeninsular Highway at Chapala. From there, you can head south to Bahía de los Angeles or turn north to Ensenada and Mexico 3, which returns to Mexicali.

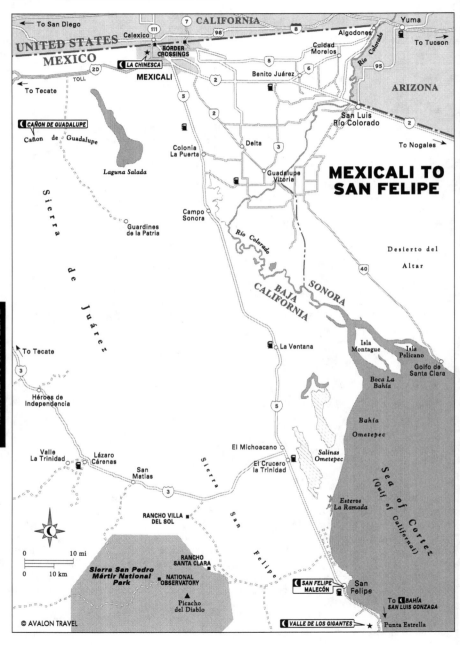

MEXICALI TO SAN FELIPE

Mexicali

Founded on March 14, 1903, Mexicali has little resemblance to its border cousins, Tecate and Tijuana. As the capital of the state of Baja California (Norte) and a major agricultural hub, most of the city's one million people are too busy to take much notice of the steady stream of tourists that make their way through Mexicali to San Felipe and points south. What the city lacks in painted donkeys and street vendors, it makes up for with efficient business hotels and fine restaurants that depend on local repeat customers. The Zona Hotelera and the area along Calle Benito Juárez offer adequate nightlife with several clubs and bars.

As a visitor to Mexicali, you can choose to blend in with the locals by catching an Aguilas baseball game, watching a bullfight, or sampling *Bajanese* cuisines in La Chinesca, Mexico's only true Chinatown. If your vacation destination is beyond the city's borders, there are several hotels that cater to the guests who view Mexicali as a border staging area with secure parking and low rates.

The nicest times to visit Mexicali are any month except the peak of summer, when temperatures regularly top 38°C.

HISTORY

The Spanish first came to the Valle de Mexicali along the Camino del Diablo (Devil's Road) in the Sonora Desert. The Yumano tribes that inhabited the area grew squash, peas, melon, and corn. They also had advanced uses for medicinal herbs and used the desert flora and fauna in a variety of ways.

The Cucapá (People of the River) were a major Yumano group who traveled the Río Colorado in reed rafts. The arrival of the Spanish reduced the numbers of Cucapás to the point that today the descendents live in a small corner of the delta. Very few indigenous customs remain.

Mexicali's emergence as an agricultural center followed irrigation of the Imperial Valley on the U.S. side of the border at the turn of the 20th century.

ALTO GOLFO DE CALIFORNIA AND DELTA DEL RÍO COLORADO

Mexicali and Calexico occupy the same valley bordered by the Colorado River delta to the east and the Sierra de Cucapá to the west. Developers renamed the valley north of the border the Imperial Valley. It's also known as the Salton Sink. South of the border, it's simply called Valle de Mexicali. The entire valley was once part of the Gulf of California, before silt from the flooding of the river pushed the shoreline to the south.

The Colorado River is the deciding geographical factor in this area. For millennia, the river flowed directly to the Gulf bounded by its own natural levees, which were built up by silt. The valley itself lay underwater. Periodically, the river would break its banks and flood the Salton Sink. Over time, the break would fill back up with silt, and the temporary Salton Sea would evaporate.

In 1905, developers lost control of an irrigation project and accidentally diverted virtually the entire flow of the Colorado River into the Salton Sink. It took a railroad company's crews several years to repair the breach and correct the river's flow.

Today, the irrigation system leftover from the early 20th-century developers continues to support a vibrant agricultural economy. But 90 percent of the Colorado River is diverted prior to reaching the border. And the All American Canal north of the border might be paved, which would prevent further seepage flows south of the border.

Los Angeles Times publisher Harry Chandler was a key figure behind the irrigation of the Valle de Mexicali on the Mexico side of the border. With Chinese immigrant laborers imported to dig its canal, Mexicali became green virtually overnight. However, a 1905 storm rerouted the entire flow of the river into the valley, flooding Mexicali and filling the Salton Sea once again.

The Southern Pacific Railroad worked for several years to route the river back into the Sea of Cortez, leaving only the original channel off the main canal.

In 1911, the Magonista faction of revolutionaries briefly took control of Mexicali. To protect the border, the Mexican government moved the capital of the Territory of Baja California to Mexicali from Ensenada. With the passage of Prohibition in the United States, Mexicali experienced an influx of tourism that was made famous by the song "Mexicali Rose." Jack Tenney wrote the lyrics, originally called "The Waltz" and claimed it wasn't about a dancing girl, but was written for an elderly bar patron. Bing Crosby recorded it before Gene Autry starred in a movie by that name. Tenney went to law school and was elected to the California State Legislature. Chinese workers who had helped build the irrigation canals opened many of the area's Prohibition-era businesses.

Baja California (Norte) became a Mexican state in 1952. Cotton was initially the cash crop in the valley, but with the invention of synthetic fibers, asparagus, green onions, and other crops became more important to the economy. The Agrobaja convention (www.agrobaja.com), held in March each year, brings 50,000 U.S. and Mexican agricultural and fishery interests to town.

With the addition of a manufacturing base in the form of in-bond plants and maquiladoras, the population of Mexicali began to rise, and has doubled since the 1970s.

Mexicali's economy remains closely tied to that of the United States, and the current economic downturn has resulted in widespread layoffs at the maquiladoras. Some forays into

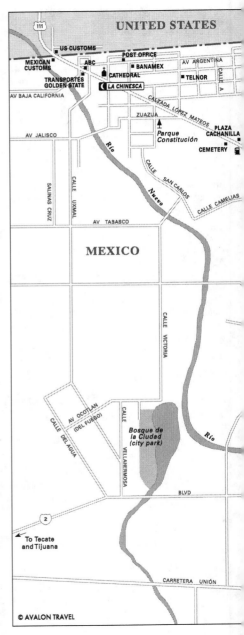

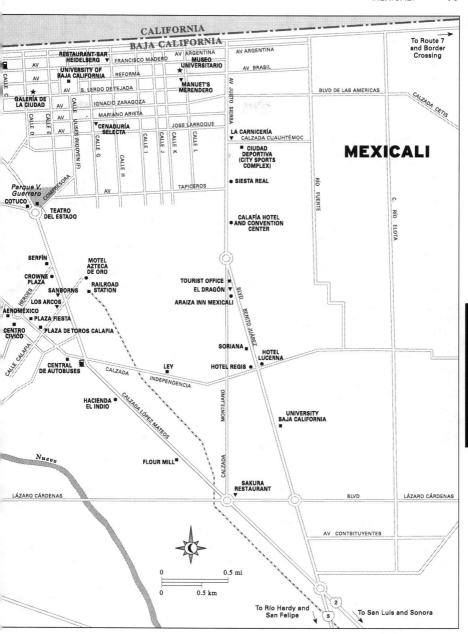

CALIFORNIA
BAJA CALIFORNIA

To Route 7
and Border
Crossing

RESTAURANT-BAR
HEIDELBERG ▼
FRANCISCO MADERO
AV ARGENTINA
AV ARGENTINA
MUSEO
UNIVERSITARIO
★
AV BRASIL
UNIVERSITY OF
BAJA CALIFORNIA
REFORMA
AV
AV
CALLE C
AV
S. LERDO DE TEJADA
MANUET'S
MERENDERO
BLVD DE LAS AMERICAS
CALZADA CETIS
★
GALERÍA DE
LA CIUDAD
AV
IGNACIO ZARAGOZA
AV
MARIANO ARISTA
CALLE D
CALLE E
AV
▼CENADURÍA
SELECTA
JOSE LARROQUE
LA CARNICERÍA
CALZADA CUAUHTÉMOC
▼
CALLE G
CALLE H
CALLE I
CALLE J
CALLE K
CALLE L
ULISES IRIGOYEN (F)
AV JUSTO SIERRA
■ CIUDAD
DEPORTIVA
(CITY SPORTS
COMPLEX)
MEXICALI
Parque V.
Guerrero
COMPRESORA
AV
TAPICEROS
● SIESTA REAL
RÍO FUERTE
C. RÍO ELOTA
COTUCO
TEATRO
DEL ESTADO
CALAFÍA HOTEL
● AND CONVENTION
CENTER
SERFÍN ●
CROWNE
PLAZA ●
MOTEL
AZTECA
DE ORO
HEROES
SANBORNS
▼
RAILROAD
STATION
TOURIST OFFICE ■
EL DRAGÓN ▼
●
BLVD. BENITO JUÁREZ
LOS ARCOS
▼
ARAIZA INN MEXICALI
AEROMÉXICO
■
PLAZA FIESTA
CENTRO
CÍVICO
PLAZA DE TOROS CALAFIA
SORIANA ■
HOTEL
LUCERNA
CALLE CALAFIA
CENTRAL
DE AUTOBUSES
CALZADA
LEY
■
INDEPENDENCIA
HOTEL REGIS ●
MONTEJANO
HACIENDA
EL INDIO
CALZADA LÓPEZ MATEOS
UNIVERSITY
BAJA CALIFORNIA
■
Nuevo
FLOUR MILL ■
CALZADA
LÁZARO CÁRDENAS
SAKURA
RESTAURANT
▼
BLVD
LÁZARO CÁRDENAS
AV CONTSITUYENTES

0   0.5 mi
0   0.5 km

To Río Hardy and
San Felipe
To San Luis and Sonora
2
5

MEXICALI TO SAN FELIPE

clean-tech industry may help the city through the cycle: Silicon Border is a company that is trying to build out a science park and manufacturing complex located to the west of Mexicali along the international border. The groundbreaking ceremony took place in 2005, but the park was without a tenant until 2008, when a solar-power manufacturer committed to moving in.

The Cerro Prieto geothermal power plant opened south of Mexicali in 1973. Today, it is one of the largest producers of geothermal power in the world. In early 2009, the company signed a deal with the City of Los Angeles to sell power from its plant.

SIGHTS
Centro Interactivo Sol del Niño

This children's museum (Blvd. López Mateos Blvd and Calle Alfonso Esquer, tel. 686/554-9595 or -9696, Mon.–Fri. 9 A.M.–7 P.M., Sat.–Sun. 10 A.M.–2 P.M., free), located in a former cotton seed warehouse, has more than 250 interactive science and technology exhibits.

◖ La Chinesca

Mexicali is home to Mexico's only distinct Chinatown. The intersection at the heart of the district is Calle Benito Juárez and Calle Altamirano close to the border crossing. The city itself boasts 100 Chinese restaurants, mostly serving Cantonese-style cuisine. Earlier in the 20th century, the percentage of Chinese residents in the city was much higher, and the only two cinemas in the city played movies in Chinese. Today, relatively few Chinese families remain, but Chinese culture and traditions live on. The signature monument to the Chinese presence in Mexicali is the pagoda on Plaza de Amistad (just outside the district). It was made entirely by Chinese craftsmen using materials shipped from China and was dedicated in 1994.

Bosque de la Ciudad

Visit Bosque de la Ciudad in southwest Mexicali (Av. Ocotlán and Calle Alvarado,

downtown Mexicali

Tues.–Sun. 9 A.M.–5 P.M.), when you need a break from the dusty downtown. This large city park has its own lake and zoo.

ENTERTAINMENT AND EVENTS
Baseball

Mexicali's professional baseball team, **Las Aguilas (The Eagles),** is part of the Mexican Pacific League and plays at El Nido de las Aguilas (Eagles' Nest) stadium, located in the **Cuidad Deportiva** (City Sports Complex, Calz. Justo Sierra, tel. 686/567-5129, www.aguilas-demexicali.com.mx, Nov.–Jan.). General admission tickets start at US$40.

Nightlife

Antrojo (Calz. Juárez 1807, tel. 686/568-2129) plays house music for a younger crowd. It's open Wednesday, Friday, and Saturday until 2 A.M. **La Capilla** is a music and dance club inside the Hotel Lucerna (Calz. Juárez 2151, tel. 686/564-7000, nightly until 2 A.M.). Bars at the Hotel Crowne Plaza, Araiza Inn Mexicali, and Araiza Inn Calafía often have live music in the evening.

Teatro del Estado (State Theater)

Baja California's state theater (tel. 686/554-6419, icbcteatrodelestado@hotmail.com) occupies a 1,100-seat venue at Calzado López Mateos and Avenida Castellanos. The city tourist office also has performance schedules (tel. 888/268-8262).

Festivals and Events

Baja Prog (www.bajaprog.org) takes place in March, with four days of progressive rock band performances. Most of the festival takes place at the Hotel Araiza, but the finale is held at the Teatro Del Estado (State Theatre) on Boulevard López Mateos.

In March or April, the **Mexicali 500** (www.codeoffroad.com.mx) off-road race starts in Mexicali and ends in San Felipe. The course follows the Laguna Salada dry lakebed.

In September–October, the **Fiesta del Sol** (Parque Vicente Guerrero, www.fiestasdelsol.com.mx) draws some 500,000 people over the course of 21 days to commemorate the founding of Mexicali in 1904. During the event, a festival queen is named and a number of cultural performances and art shows provide entertainment.

In November, the local chamber of restaurants, CANIRAC, holds **Muestra Gastronómica,** a food fair featuring Mexican, seafood, and Chinese cuisines (tel. 686/554-3285, www.caniracnacional.com.mx, canirac-1mexicali@prodigy.net.mx).

On Sunday afternoons, mariachi groups often play at **Parque Constitución,** a park at Avenida Hidalgo and Calle Aldama.

SHOPPING

Unless you're buying agricultural supplies or prescription medication, the visitor-oriented shopping is limited in Mexicali. The border zone along Calle Melgar has the usual shops selling kitschy souvenirs. **Plaza Cataviña** (Calz. Cetys 1800, Col. Cataviña, tel. 686/567-2896) caters to the young, upscale crowd with

a modern health club and a variety of electronics, clothing, and jewelry stores.

El Armario (Calz. Justo Sierra 1700 at Blvd. Juárez, Plaza Azteca, tel. 686/568-1906) has rustic Mexican furniture, glassware, and handicrafts.

Plaza Cachanilla (Calz. López Mateos, northwest of Parque Vicente Guerrero, tel. 686/553-4177 or -4108) is a huge mall located just a few minutes away from the international border. In the summer, when the weather is hot, local families will come and spend the day inside the cool shopping mall.

ACCOMMODATIONS

Mexicali accommodations cost less than their counterparts in Tijuana and Ensenada. If you shop around when you arrive, you can often get much lower rates than if you make reservations ahead of time. The higher-end hotels cater to Mexican business travelers with meeting rooms and business centers. On the less-expensive end of the spectrum, there are a number of hotels that supply visitors with functional rooms, off-street parking, and air-conditioning.

Under US$50

Motel Reforma (Av. Reforma 625, tel. 686/533-6831, US$30) caters to budget travelers looking for accommodations near the border. It's slightly better than the **Hotel San Juan Capistrano** (Av. Reforma 646, tel. 686/552-4104, US$30) a few doors down. As you head west of boulevard López Mateos, the motels get cheaper, but they are real dives.

Motel Azteca de Oro (Calle de la Industria 600, tel. 686/557-1433, www.hotelaztecadeoro.com, US$42–60) is a typical two-story motel with air-conditioned rooms, but six rooms are combined with a private enclosed one-car garage. The rooms are standard for the price range, with older beds and shabby bathrooms. Two-story **Hotel Hacienda del Indio** (Calz. López Mateos 101 at Av. Fresnillo, tel. 686/557-2277, US$45) has 50 recently renovated rooms that surround an enclosed courtyard. **Hotel Regis** (Calz. Juárez 2150, tel. 686/566-8801, www.hotel-regis.com, US$45) is another good choice for clean, basic rooms.

US$50-100

If you're simply stopping over on your way south, or looking for a base from which to launch a fishing or hunting trip, the **Hotel Siesta Real** (Calz. Justo Sierra 899, tel. 686/568-2001, toll-free U.S. tel. 800/426-5093, www.hotelsiestareal.com, US$48–80) is a convenient option. Its 90 rooms have air-conditioning, TVs, and phones. Guests may also use a swimming pool, restaurant, and off-street parking lot.

Hotel Posada Inn (Blvd. López Mateos 939 at Calle Torneros, tel. 686/558-6100, www.hotelposadainn.com, US$63) has wireless Internet, air-conditioned rooms, off-street parking in a courtyard, and a nice sitting area on the upper walkway. It's situated on the east side of a partitioned road, so it can be difficult to get in and out by car.

The **Calafia Hotel and Convention Center** (Calz. Justo Sierra 1495, tel. 686/568-3311 or 800/026-5444, U.S. tel. 877/727-2492, www.araizainn.com.mx, US$79) houses the Calafía Steakhouse and a separate sports bar. Part of the Araiza chain, it is a clean, four-story motel with 170 rooms. The hotel caters to traveling families with a pool and secure parking. It is located next to a police station.

US$100-150

South of the Calafía along the same boulevard (which changes names en route), the **Araiza Inn Mexicali** (Calz. Juárez 2220, tel. 686/564-1100 or 800/686-5444, U.S. tel. 877/727-2492, www.araizainn.com.mx, US$70–120) has 190 rooms. The Fonda restaurant is often packed. Some of the suites have been renovated and are very nice, with flat-screen TVs, shoe-buffing machines, and spinning cycles. This hotel also has a swimming pool, coffee shop, bar, and disco.

Hotel Lucerna (Calz. Juárez 2151, tel. 686/564-7000, US$106) has 176 rooms each with air-conditioning, minibar, satellite TV, and phone. There are two pools, a fitness center, and the Restaurant Mezzosole. The tower you see when you turn left out of the reception office is worn out. For the best accommodations, ask for a bungalow. They were newly renovated, and have the feel of a W Hotel room. The family suite has a separate bedroom, spinning cycle, bathrobes, and two flat-screen TVs. Also note, this hotel has limited secured parking.

The **Fiesta Inn Mexicali** (Calz. López Mateos 1029, tel. 686/837-3300, www.fiestainn.com, US$83–135) is a newly built hotel with more than 150 rooms in a multistory white building. It's located a few minutes from the border, across from the city's bullfighting arena, and within striking distance of several shopping malls.

The **Crowne Plaza** (Blvd. López Mateos at Av. de los Héroes, tel. 686/557-3600, toll-free U.S. tel. 800/227-6963, www.crowneplaza.com, US$100–150) has most of the same amenities as the Araiza and Fiesta chains. A sports bar features pool tables and a widescreen TV. Nonsmoking rooms are available.

FOOD

Mexicali has a less-developed food scene than Tijuana or Ensenada, but it does have its own signature cuisine, Mexicali-Chinese, and plenty of places to find an enjoyable meal.

Chinese

At last count, there were just under 100 Chinese restaurants in Mexicali. The cooking is mostly Cantonese, but Mexicali-Chinese has evolved into a unique cuisine. For example, a bowl of ketchup-like sauce is commonly served as a condiment. You may also be served a bowl of jalapenos with soy sauce, limes, and salt.

Dragón (Av. Libertad 990, tel. 686/557-4425, daily for lunch and dinner, mains US$10) is an upscale Cantonese restaurant that can hold several hundred diners. The signature dish here is duck with mushrooms. Another good choice is **Fortune House** (Lázaro Cárdenas 1153, tel. 686/555-8848, daily 11 A.M.–11 P.M., mains US$10) near the exit to Mexico 2 and Tijuana.

Other International

Close to downtown, **Restaurant-Bar Heidelberg** (Av. Madero at Calle H, tel. 686/554-2022, http://restauranteheidelberg.com/index.html, Mon.–Sat. noon–1 A.M., mains US$15–25) offers German and Continental fare. The atmosphere is pleasant, but prices are high. With an attached piano bar, **Restaurant Italiano Mandolino** (Av. Reforma 1070, tel. 686/552-9544, daily for lunch and dinner, mains US$10–15) has long been popular for Italian cuisine.

Mexicali has a good option for sushi as well: **Sakura Restaurant** (Blvd. Lázaro Cárdenas 2004 at Calz. Montejano, tel. 686/566-0514 or -4848, Tues–Sun. 8 A.M.–midnight, mains US$10–15) serves teppanyaki and sushi with the **Karaoke Video Bar** upstairs.

Mexican

In a former American-style drive-in, **Merendero Manuet's** (Calle L at Av. Pino Suárez, tel. 686/552-5694, daily 10 A.M.–1 A.M., mains US$5–10) has a full menu of *antojitos* and a full bar occupied by local ranchers and farmers in cowboy hats. The waitresses waited on the parents of some of the younger patrons that drink beer and smoke in the parking lots on weekends.

Another option for *antojitos* was brand new at press time: **Mr. Choby's** (Blvd. Benito Juárez 1199 at Calle Carranza, no tel., Sun.–Thurs. noon–10 P.M., Fri.–Sat. 10 A.M.–1 A.M.), in the Las Villas food court. Full *botana* platters go for US$22, while individual mains start at US$5. **Fonda de Mexicali** (Juárez 2220, tel. 686/564-1100 ext. 721, mains US$15 and up) in the Hotel Araiza does a huge brunch buffet on Sundays for US$15. The food is a notch above the typical hotel restaurant fare.

In business since 1945, **La Cenaduría Selecta** (Av. Arista 1510 at Calle G, Col. Nueva, tel. 686/552-4047, Mon. 7 A.M.–5 P.M., Tues.–Sun. 8 A.M.–11 P.M., mains US$12 and up) is best known for its *mole* dishes.

◖ **La Carnicería** (Panamá 190 at Calz. Justo Sierra, Col. Cuauhtémoc, tel. 686/568-101, daily for lunch and dinner, mains

tacos on the outskirts of Mexicali

US$18) is an elegant steakhouse that features an indoor grill and brick oven behind glass. Try the mini *al pastor* tacos to start and the very good Queso Fondido fondue platter. There is a bar attached to the restaurant with modern decor and live music occasionally on the weekends.

Seafood

◖ **Los Arcos Restaurant/Bar** (Calafía 454, tel. 686/556-0903, www.restaurantlosarcos.com.mx, Mon.–Thurs. 11 A.M.–10 P.M., Fri.–Sun. 11 A.M.–11 P.M., mains US$10–15) is part of a chain of 14 restaurants scattered throughout Mexico. Located in the Centro Cívico district, it is the best place in town for fresh seafood.

Groceries

The warehouse-style **Soriana** (Blvd. Juárez north of Independencia), near the Hotel Lucerna, and 24-hour **Ley**, on Independencia or at Plaza Fiesta on Calzada López Mateos, are your best options for stocking up on food and supplies. There is a Costco (Carr. San Luis-Río Colorado, Km 7.5, tel. 686/580-4530, daily 9 A.M.–9 P.M.) on the road out of town as you drive on Mexico 5 toward San Felipe.

INFORMATION AND SERVICES
Tourist Assistance

The Mexicali Tourism and Convention Bureau (COTUCO) has offices on Boulevard López Mateos at Calle Camelias (tel. 686/552-4401 or 888/342-7323, www.mexicaliturismo.com, Mon.–Fri. 8 A.M.–7 P.M.). The information counter has friendly and helpful staff who speak English.

The state tourism department, SECTUR, also has an office in town, at Boulevard Benito Juárez 1 and Calzada Montejano (tel. 686/566-1161 or 686/558-1000, Mon.–Fri. 8 A.M.–5 P.M., Sat.–Sun. 10 A.M.–3 P.M.). The state's legal assistance department (Attorney for Tourist Protection, tel./fax 686/566-1116) is based here as well.

Money

Banks are numerous in Mexicali. Banamex, Bancomer, and Serfín each have multiple branches, most with ATMs. If you need to exchange currency, the banks offer this service only until about noon each day. Numerous *casas de cambio* on both sides of the border are another option.

Post and Telephone

Mexicali's main post and a Western Union office are located at Calzada Independencia and Calle Pioneros (Mon.–Fri. 8 A.M.–3 P.M., Sat. 9 A.M.–1 P.M.). But it's probably better to mail your postcards across the border in Calexico on Birch Street and George Avenue, four blocks west of Imperial Avenue.

Long-distance Ladatel phones can be found throughout Mexicali. Check the rate before you dial an international number. Many U.S. mobile phones continue to pick up a signal across the border into Mexicali. Beyond this zone, you'll need to set yourself up for international roaming (call your service provider before you go). Mobile phones that use the international GSM standard are the only ones that can connect reliably throughout Baja California.

Mexican Consulate

For information about immigration paperwork for traveling into Mexico, including vehicle import permits for driving on the mainland, visit the Mexican consulate on the U.S side of the border in Calexico (331 W. Second St., U.S. tel. 760/357-3863, fax 760/357-6284, Mon.–Fri. 8 A.M.–3 P.M.).

Border Crossing

The main (west) Mexicali border crossing stays open around the clock, every day. The crowds here will be considerably thinner than the crossing at Tijuana, but lines do back up during the morning and afternoon commutes. East of the main crossing, a second gateway joins Calexico East with Mexicali's industrial zone (daily 6 A.M.–10 P.M.). Wait times here are typically less half the time at the main crossing; however, if your ultimate destination is

San Diego or other points west, you'll spend a good amount of time circling east and back around to the west.

If you are a hunter coming back to the United States with game to declare, use the east crossing; the border officials at the main crossing may not know how to handle the paperwork.

If you're traveling south of Mexicali, you'll need a tourist permit, which you can pick up at the Oficina de Federal building that's marked *Migracion* or *Aduana* located to the left of the border gates as you pass through from the U.S. side.

GETTING THERE
By Air
Mexicali has an international airport, **Aeropuerto Internacional General Rodolfo Sánchez Taboada** (MXL), 20 kilometers east of the city via Boulevard de las Américas. No U.S. airlines currently serve the airport, but **Aeroméxico** (Pasaje Alamos 1008-D, Centro Cívico Comercial, tel. 686/557-2551) and **Mexicana** (Av. Obregón, tel. 686/553-5401) offer connections from Hermosillo, Sonora, on the mainland. Mexicana also flies to/from Guadalajara, Monterrey, and Mexico City.

A taxi from the airport to downtown Mexicali runs about US$15.

By Car
From the San Diego airport, take I-5 north to I-8 past El Centro, and take Route 111 south to the border. This route takes about two hours. There is parking on the Calexico side of the border at **Double AA Parking** (201 W. Second St., U.S. tel. 760/357-3213) or **Calexico Parking & Storage** (465 W. Second St., tel. 760/357-2477, Mon.–Fri. 6 A.M.–6 P.M.), where you can also store your vehicle (US$1.50/day) or trailer (US$3/day).

After passing through the border patrol, you'll reach a Y in the road. Stay right. The toll crossing is in the middle of town itself, with the usual insurance companies, fast food restaurants, and money exchangers lining the last few blocks on the U.S. side.

To reach the east crossing, take I-8 to Route 7 south. For current border wait times, visit http://apps.cbp.gov/bwt/.

Mexicali's main north–south roads are well marked. The smaller streets running north–south are named by letters in the alphabet starting with A near Route 111 and descending as you head east.

By Bus
Mexicali's **Central de Autobuses** (on the south side of Calz. Independencia btw Calz. López Mateos/Centro Cívico, tel. 686/557-2410 or -2450) offers intercity connections to Baja and the mainland. **ABC** (Tijuana tel. 664/683-5681, www.abc.com.mx) offers connections to Mexicali from Ensenada and Tijuana. **Estrellas del Pacífico** (Tijuana tel. 664/683-5022 or -6789) also runs buses to/from Mexicali and Ensenada. **Transportes Norte de Sonora** (TNS), **Transportes del Pacífico,** and **Elite** provide connections to the mainland.

To reach the bus terminal via public transportation, catch a local Calle 6 bus from one of the stops along Calzada López Mateos.

The small ABC terminal on López Mateos (btw Azueta/Madero) offers frequent service to Tecate, Tijuana, and Ensenada.

The **Greyhound** station in Calexico (123 First St., U.S. tel. 760/357-1895), right at the pedestrian border crossing, runs direct connections to San Diego and Los Angeles. From the Calexico depot, you walk across through the border gate and take a taxi to Mexicali bus depot (under US$10).

GETTING AROUND
By Bus
Mexicali's city buses are signed for their final destination (e.g., Centro Cívico, Justo Sierra). Many of these bus routes originate on Calle Altamirano downtown, close to the border crossing. Fares are less than US$1.

By Taxi
Taxis de ruta (route taxis) cover many of the same routes for a slightly higher fare. Private

taxi fare runs about US$5 downtown, US$6–8 to/from the border to the Centro Cívico area or the Boulevard Juárez hotel zone. Aside from the pedestrian border crossing, the larger hotels are good places to find an available taxi. To order a taxi, call **Radio Taxis Cervantes** (tel. 686/568-3718) or **Ecotaxi** (tel. 686/562-6565).

By Car

Aside from its many traffic circles, called *glorietas,* Mexicali is a fairly easy city to navigate by car. Street parking is readily available.

Follow Calle Juárez to find Mexico 5 south to San Felipe. There are several ways to get to Mexico 2, which goes east to Sonora and west to Tecate and Tijuana.

Pemex stations are easy to find, and these days, most offer Premium fuel.

MEXICO 5 SOUTH TO SAN FELIPE

If you want to proceed directly to Mexico 5 south toward San Felipe from the main border crossing (Route 111), keep to your right as you approach the border booths. Stop for the border light, which will flash either green or red. If it's green, you can continue. If it's red, you will need to pull over for further inspection. If you need to get a tourist visa or have an FM3 stamped, the immigration office is on the immediate right.

As you cross the border, bear to your right to get onto Boulevard López Mateos. Continue past the first traffic circle with the statue of Ignacio Allende. Get into the right-hand lane and follow the signs to San Felipe as the road forks to the right and you cross the railroad tracks. At the next traffic circle, follow the signs to San Felipe, and then take a left at the next light. This road will turn into Mexico 5 and will take you all the way into San Felipe.

Coming from the new border crossing to the east, the road will end in a T a few hundred

Mexico 5, north of San Felipe

© PAUL ITOI

meters from the border. Go right at the T, then take a left onto Boulevard Gomez Morin. This will take you straight to Mexico 5. Stay in the middle of the three lanes to avoid most of the abrupt stops.

The drive is mostly flat, but you'll have plenty to look at as you go from farmland to lakebed to desert. About an hour and half into the drive you can often see the Gulf of California in the distance. As you get closer to San Felipe, you'll encounter construction crews that are widening the road from two lanes to four. Eventually, the entire stretch from Mexicali to San Felipe with be four lanes.

The total drive time from the border to San Felipe is around two hours. For the return trip north, add at least one hour to make sure you have enough time to cross the border. During rush hour, or on holidays, the border wait can be several hours.

Mexicali to Tecate

West of Mexicali, Mexico 2 follows the northern foothills of the Sierra de los Cucapá and the top of **Laguna Salada,** a 100-kilometer-long dry salt lake. The Pemex station near Km 24 is the only option for fuel until La Rumorosa (53 km farther west). If you drive along Mexico 2-D between Mexicali and Tecate, you'll pass through two toll booths, each of which costs approximately US$2.50.

After Laguna Salada, the highway ascends the Sierra de Juárez, where several palm canyons named Tajo, El Carrizo, Guadalupe, and El Palomar offer prime hiking, off-roading, and wilderness camping. Spring-fed streams run year-round, but the time to go is between November and April. From May to October, the temperatures can get above 38°C.

◖ CAÑON DE GUADALUPE

Of the four larger canyons in this part of the Sierra de Juárez, 400-hectare Cañon de Guadalupe is the most popular among hikers and campers because of its healing hot springs. In this high-elevation oasis, granite peaks tower over a sea of blue fan palms. Waterfalls, prehistoric rock art, and solar power all are part of the experience.

Camping

Guadalupe Canyon Hot Springs and Campground (U.S. tel. 949/673-2670, www.guadalupe-canyon.com, US$50–75) is divided into two campgrounds: Arturo's Campo and Los Manantiales (Mario's Campo). The same family owns the entire valley and so far has resisted having it developed. In 2007, a fire burned most of the property, but it's in the process of being rebuilt. Arturo's campsites are arranged to afford more privacy. Each of the eight campsites features its own private hot tub made of river rock and cement, and you can adjust the temperature between 26–41°C. The sites can accommodate multiple vehicles, and there is a two-night minimum on weekends and a three-night minimum on holiday weekends. Pets are welcome, with proof of vaccinations.

Facilities for campers include outhouses, showers, and a market that sells the basics. Refrigeration is provided by 45-kilogram blocks of ice. The owners do not want you to collect firewood or disturb any of the natural surroundings, but firewood is for sale. The canyon is popular on the holidays and the weekends, so book early.

Guided Hikes

For tours of the Cañon de Guadalupe, contact **Rupestres** (mobile tel. 044/686/158-9921, www.rupestres.com, explorandobajacalifornia@hotmail.com, US$70).

Getting There

From Mexicali, take Calle Guadalajara about eight kilometers south to Mexico 2 West and follow the highway for 32 kilometers. The first turn is labeled Cañon de Guadalupe and Laguna Salada. The road is available only from the eastbound lanes, so you'll need to pass the intersection and double back at the next U-turn opportunity. This first turn is faster and more direct, but because it uses the dry lakebed of the Laguna Salada for 40 kilometers, it will be muddy and impassable following any rain. When you drive across the lakebed, don't worry if there are multiple tracks. Follow the most worn route and keep heading south/southwest and look for the occasional sign to the canyon. If you're not comfortable navigating the lakebed, you can take the second turnoff which is 4.3 kilometers farther west and also labeled Cañon de Guadalupe. This road has a higher elevation, so it's less vulnerable to rain, but it takes longer (about 45 minutes to go 43 km) and is a less comfortable ride. Both roads merge at the opening of the canyon. The rest of the drive is increasingly winding and rocky—recommended only for high-clearance vehicles.

Eleven kilometers from the main road, a

very rocky few hundred meters will bring you to the campground entrance.

LA RUMOROSA AND VICINITY

Heading west from Mexicali, at around Km 44, the highway climbs the steep Juárez escarpment to the town of La Rumorosa. Named for the whispering winds that blow by the 1,275-meter pass, the village is populated with the summer homes of Mexicali and Tijuana residents. The old highway was infamous for the number of fatal accidents. After the old road was closed, it was used in the filming of a James Bond movie. La Rumorosa's most famous resident might be El Diablito (Little Devil). He is a small red figure painted in a cave in the nearby El Vallecito. Only on December 21, the winter solstice, a ray of sunlight illuminates the figure. The **Museo Camp Alaska** (no tel., hours vary) is located in the middle of town in an old stone garrison and contains the history of the indigenous people of the area. For tours of El Vallecito and La Rumorosa, contact **Rupestres** (mobile tel. 044/686/158-9921, www.rupestres.com, explorandobajacalifornia@hotmail.com, US$60).

Food

Restaurant Asadero El Chipo (no tel., daily for lunch and dinner) on Mexico 2 at the west end of town serves excellent tacos for less than US$2 each.

Laguna Hanson

At Km 73, west of La Rumorsa, there is a graded dirt road that leads 63 kilometers to Laguna Hanson in the Parque Nacional Constitución de 1857. The second half of the road is for high-clearance vehicles only; four-wheel drive is recommended. The park is more easily approached via Mexico 3, southeast of Ensenada.

San Felipe and Vicinity

San Felipe (pop. 25,000) is a small coastal town on the Sea of Cortez, about two hours' drive south of the U.S./Mexico border. California and Arizona residents flock here for weekend RV and fishing trips. Punta San Felipe protects the bay from north winds. To get oriented, begin your trip by climbing the stairs to the top of the 240-meter **Cerro El Machorro** located on the point. You'll see a shrine to the Virgin of Guadalupe and panoramic views of the bay.

In the 1940s and '50s, American fishermen came down to catch the abundant *totuava,* a sporting croaker that could reach up to 115 kilograms. The tasty fish proved to be too popular and it's now on the endangered species list and off limits for any fishing. San Felipe faces a similar clash of supply and demand today. Recent fishing and shrimping practices have endangered a rare breed of small porpoise called the *vaquita.* The Zoological Society of London has designated it as one of the 100 EDGE species (Evolutionarily Distinct, Globally Endangered), which makes it a top priority for conservationists. There is a monument to the *vaquita* at the center of the *malecón* in San Felipe.

More than 250,000 tourists visit San Felipe annually. The populated area around San Felipe stretches for quite a few kilometers of coastline to the north and south. Besides fishing, there are sand dunes for ATVs and dune buggies, which are a common site around town.

The town has a splash of nightlife along the *malecón* with several clubs, bars, and the periodic S.W.A.T invasion. S.W.A.T is a tour company that brings in busloads of college students during spring break and throughout the year for all-inclusive party weekends.

Most visitors choose the months of November–April to visit the area. The temperatures are generally milder than Mexicali in the summer months, but they can still often break 38°C.

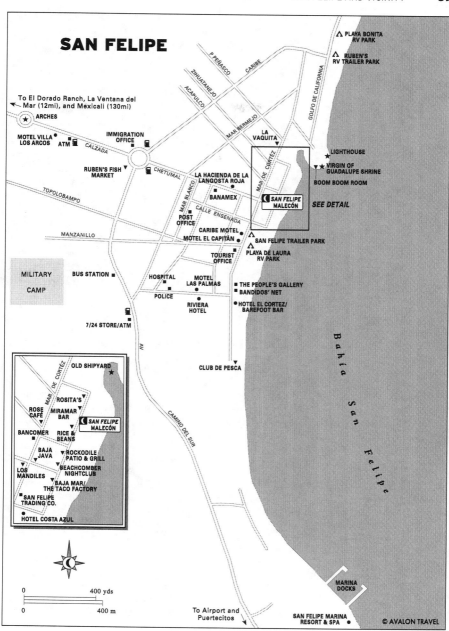

SAN FELIPE

To El Dorado Ranch, La Ventana del
← Mar (12mi), and Mexicali (130mi)

★ ARCHES

MOTEL VILLA
LOS ARCOS   ATM   CALZADA

IMMIGRATION
OFFICE

RUBEN'S FISH
MARKET

CHETUMAL

TOPOLOBAMPO

MANZANILLO

MILITARY
CAMP

BUS STATION ■

HOSPITAL

POLICE

7/24 STORE/ATM

P PEÑASCO

ZIHUATANEJO

ACAPULCO

CARIBE

MAR BERMEJO

LA
VAQUITA

LA HACIENDA DE LA
LANGOSTA ROJA

BANAMEX

MAR BLANCO

CALLE ENSENADA

POST
OFFICE

CARIBE MOTEL
MOTEL EL CAPITÁN ●

TOURIST
OFFICE

MOTEL
LAS PALMAS

RIVIERA
HOTEL

MAR DE CORTEZ

SAN FELIPE
MALECÓN

SEE DETAIL

▲ SAN FELIPE TRAILER PARK

▲ PLAYA DE LAURA
RV PARK

■ THE PEOPLE'S GALLERY
■ BANDIDOS' NET

● HOTEL EL CORTEZ/
BAREFOOT BAR

CLUB DE PESCA ▼

GOLFO DE CALIFORNIA

▲ PLAYA BONITA
RV PARK

▲ RUBEN'S
RV TRAILER PARK

LIGHTHOUSE

▼ ★ VIRGIN OF
GUADALUPE SHRINE

BOOM BOOM ROOM

B a h í a

S a n

F e l i p e

DETAIL (inset)

MAR DE CORTEZ

OLD SHIPYARD ★

ROSITA'S ▼

ROSE
CAFÉ

MIRAMAR
BAR

BANCOMER

RICE &
BEANS

SAN FELIPE
MALECÓN

BAJA
JAVA

▼ ROCKODILE
PATIO & GRILL

▼ BEACHCOMBER
NIGHTCLUB

LOS
MANDILES

BAJA MAR/
THE TACO FACTORY

■ SAN FELIPE
TRADING CO.

HOTEL COSTA AZUL ●

CAMINO DEL SUR

AV

N

0   400 yds
0   400 m

MARINA
DOCKS

To Airport and
Puertecitos ↓

SAN FELIPE MARINA
RESORT & SPA ●

© AVALON TRAVEL

© PAUL ITOI

glassblower on the *malecón*

⒞ SAN FELIPE *MALECÓN*

Public life in San Felipe centers around the *malecón*. This waterfront promenade is a smaller version of the one in La Paz and similar to Loreto's in size. There are several bars and nightclubs that offer a scaled-down version of the Rosarito beach scene. Several restaurants and shops also line the strip. Playa San Felipe stretches the length of the *malecón* and is popular with sunbathers and **pangueros** for hire.

SPORTS AND RECREATION
Fishing

Even though you'll hear seasoned area fisherman pine for the good old days, the San Felipe fishing scene is still the big draw—for visitors and retirees alike. Croakers can be found year-round, but the peak months for cabrilla, yellowtail, sierra, and grouper are May–October. Head north above Punta San Felipe for the best onshore fishing. You can still fish from shore without a license, so all you need is a shore rod, food and water, and some lures.

There are multi-day trips available to the Midriff islands 400 kilometers to the south. These trips are usually six-day fishing marathons and involve large 100-foot-plus fishing vessels. The term "mothership fishing" refers to the 6–10 *pangas* that the larger vessels carry with them. It takes around 24 hours to reach the fishing grounds from San Felipe. From there, the *pangas* typically head out with three anglers each for a morning and afternoon run. Everyone pitches in to make bait during the night.

Tony Reyes Fishing Tours (Av. Mar Bermejo 130, tel. 686/577-1120, www. tonyreyes.com) and **Baja Sportfishing** (tel. 800/770-2341, bajasportfishinginc.net) operate these long-range trips. Prices for the week run US$1,200–1,500 and include everything but tip, drinks, and tackle.

Boating

You can launch your own boat at the Motel El Cortez, Ruben's Trailer Park, or the San Felipe Marina. **Baja Directions** (www.bajadirections. com) has an updated and detailed atlas for the

Baja sportfishing areas including boat ramps, bathymetry, and gas stations.

Golf

Las Caras de Mexico Golf Course (tel. 686/576-0517, www.lascarasdemexico.com) is an 18-hole, 7,200-yard course that opened in 2005. It's part of the El Dorado Ranch and La Ventana del Mar developments. Greens fee are US$30–85 and carts are complimentary. No need to pack your clubs; you can rent a pro bag of TaylorMades (US$30/18 holes, US$15/9 holes). The turn for La Ventana del Mar is 11 kilometers north of San Felipe at Km 176.5. A mountain course on the other side of highway is under construction.

ENTERTAINMENT AND EVENTS
Nightlife

Partying in San Felipe boils down to three main choices: Rockodile, Beachcomber, or the Boom Boom Room. **Rockodile** (Ave. Mar de Cortez 199, tel. 686/577-1219, www.4rockodile.com, rockodilemexico@aol.com, daily noon–3 A.M.) is the most popular for spring-breakers, with nearly 1,500 square meters of bars, multi-level dance floors, and a soap machine that froths the willing crowd into a slippery frenzy. **Beachcomber** (Malecón/Calz. Chetumal, tel. 686/577-1670 or 686/577-1219, www.4beachcomber.com, daily noon–3 A.M.) features live pop rock and Sinaloan bands, DJs, and professional sports broadcast on the club's 60-inch screens. The enormous **Boom Boom Room** (Calle Guaymas, northern end of the *malecón,* across the footbridge that leads to the Shrine of Guadalupe, no tel., daily noon–3 A.M.) features a high-tech sound system and stunning views.

For a less caffeinated experience, grab a drink at the relatively quiet **Club Miramar** (Av. Mar de Cortez, tel. 686/577-1192, daily 10 A.M.–3 A.M.), a San Felipe classic at the north end of the *malecón.* To get away from the crowds, head south of the *malecón* to the Hotel El Cortez's **Barefoot Bar** (tel. 686/577-1055) and enjoy the tranquil view of the sea over a cold margarita.

Festivals and Events

February and March are busy months on the San Felipe events calendar. Like Ensenada and La Paz, San Felipe celebrates **Carnaval,** usually in late February or early March. The **Tecate SCORE San Felipe 250** off-road race take place in March. The **Hobie Cat Midwinters West Regatta** (midwinterswest@cox.net, February or March) is a catamaran race on Bahía de San Felipe. U.S. college students take over the town during the latter part of March for **spring break.** Steer clear unless you want to partake in the madness.

June 1 brings a national **Navy Day** (Día de la Marina Nacional); the celebration includes a street festival with live music and dancing.

SHOPPING

Run by Steve and Linda Sullivan, **The People's Gallery** (Av. Mar de Cortés Sur 381, tel. 686/577-2898, daily 10 A.M.–5 P.M.), sells the works of local artists, including handmade furniture, jewelry, masks, paintings, and other crafts. The owners also publish the informative *San Felipe Newsletter* (sfnewsster@gmail.com).

For new and used books, try the **San Felipe Trading Company** (Av. Mar de Cortés, across from the IMSS clinic and half a block north of the Costa Azul, no tel.), or a new bookstore called **The New Bookstore** (Calzada Chetumal, no tel.), one block west of the Chinese restaurant.

ACCOMMODATIONS AND CAMPING

Given its proximity to the U.S. border, San Felipe has historically had pricier accommodations than similar Baja fishing towns. Outside of the peak months (Nov.–Apr.) though, prices may be as much as 30 percent lower. Rates shown here do not include 12 percent hotel tax or 10 percent service charge, unless specified.

US$50-100

Repeat guests continue to report satisfactory stays with the clean, friendly, and safe **Chapala** (Av. Mar de Cortés 142, tel. 686/577-1240,

US$60). It's a no-frills place, but you can't beat the price. A short walk from the beach, **Motel El Capitán** (Av. Mar de Cortés 298, tel./fax 686/577-1303, U.S. tel. 866/540-7370, www. motelcapitan.com, bsfa7@prodigy.net.mx, US$75) has 45 clean rooms on two levels surrounding a parking lot and pool. Amenities include air-conditioning and TV.

Two blocks from the beach, **La Hacienda de la Langosta Roja** (Red Lobster, Calz. Chetumal 125, tel. 686/577-0483 or 800/967-0005, www.sanfelipelodging.com, US$85) is now managed by the El Dorado Ranch. The 39 rooms in this pink two-story building were recently re-furnished, but they still feel a little Motel 6. Amenities include air-conditioning and satellite TV with 15 channels. Ask for a room in the front building.

Next to Bandodos' Net, **Hotel El Cortez** (Av. Mar de Cortés, tel. 686/577-1055 or 686/577-1056, hotelcortez1@prodigy.net.mx, US$85) has 112 basic rooms facing the beach. Take a look at one before you commit. The facilities here are in much better shape than the rooms themselves, which need an overhaul and more thorough day-to-day maintenance. The hotel has a swimming pool, boat launch, laundry facilities, *palapas,* and the Barefoot Bar. Its 112 rustic rooms come with air-conditioning, TVs, and phones.

The **Caribe Motel** (Av. Mar de Cortés at Calle Ensenada, US$40–80) opened in 2008, across from the Costa Azul, with 15 rooms. Those on the front side have decks and cost more. The motel is designed in a courtyard style, with two levels. Guestrooms are upstairs and off-street, plus there is secure parking below (each spot gets it's own light). Vinyl curtains and tile floors make for harsh acoustics, but the rooms are large and come with cable TV and air-conditioning. Hot-water issues were still being worked on when we visited.

US$100-150

San Felipe Marina Resort and Spa (Km 4.5, tel. 686/577-1569 or 800/025-6925, toll-free U.S. tel. 800/291-5397, www.sanfelipemarina. net, US$144), farther south off Avenida Camino del Sur, has rooms with kitchenettes decorated in bright colors and simple furnishings, but it's not a resort in the five-star sense. Rooms are well worn, and amenities include only TV with limited channels and phones. Wi-Fi, for an extra charge, works from the lobby only. On the premises are two swimming pools (indoor and outdoor, not heated in winter), tennis courts, a restaurant/bar, and spa that doesn't seem to offer any treatments. Service is inconsistent—sometimes attentive and others times sorely lacking. The beach is the best part about a stay here.

Overlooking the sea on the road to Puertecitos, **Las Casitas Beach and Tennis Resort** (Km 1.6, 686/577-1195 or 686/187-9422, U.S. tel. 877/270-2272, www.lascasitas.com.mx, US$110–130) has air-conditioned bungalows and studios with king-size beds and private decks.

Vacation Rentals

Condominiums Playa Bonita (U.S. tel. 626/967-8977, www.sanfelipebeachcondos. com, US$60–125) has eight one-bedroom units on the beach and an adjoining RV park.

North of town, the gated **El Dorado Ranch** (tel. 686/576-0402, U.S. tel. 877/787-2624, www.eldoradoranch.com) development often has vacation rentals available in different sizes and at varying price points. Residents and guests may use community's tennis club, restaurant/bar, *palapas,* heated pool, and hot tub. The new **La Ventana del Mar** (U.S. tel. 877/787-2624, www.laventanadelmar.com, two-bedroom units US$260–310 per night) has several two- and three-bedroom units complete and available for rent.

Camping and RV Parks

Condo developments have taken over some of San Felipe's largest campgrounds in recent years. More than 20 campgrounds remain, but of these, few, if any, are designed with big rigs in mind. Amenities are often lacking, and you'll have to battle the permanent and monthly renters to get a spot. In summer, the parks that are located along the beach north of Punta San Felipe, tend to stay cooler than those on Bahía

San Felipe. A signature feature of the nicer San Felipe campgrounds are the *palapa* structures that provide a shady kitchen area underneath and a lookout deck on top. You can park your small RV under the structure, or larger ones beside it. **Playa Bonita RV Park** (tel. 686/577-1215, U.S. tel. 626/967-8977, www.sanfelipebeach-condos.com, playabonita@aol.com, US$20–40 for full hookups), and **Ruben's RV Trailer Park** (Av. Golfo de California 703, tel. 686/577-1442, US$20, full hookups only) both offer this type of *palapa* for their guests.

North of town, past the El Dorado resort, **Big RV's Camp** (Km 174–175, Mexico 5, U.S. tel. 760/427-6469, US$10–15 per night) can accommodate big rigs with full hookups. **Pete's Camp** (Km 178, Mexico 5, U.S. tel. 951/694-6704, www.petescamp.com) has 79 sites, but no hookups, for US$15. **Playa del Sol** (Km 182.5, Mexico 5, tel. 686/576-0292, US$10–15) has *palapa*-shaded tent and RV sites that overlook the beach. Limited amenities include the proximity to El Sol restaurant (Wed.–Sun., mains US$5–10), which serves Mexican staples for lunch and dinner.

Budget camping options nearby include **Marco's** (Av. Golfo de California 788, off Av. Mar de Caribe, tel. 686/577-1875 or -1842) and **Vista del Mar** (Av. Mar de Cortés 601, tel. 686/577-1252), at US$10–15 per vehicle. The tradeoff is you won't be on the beach.

South of town, long-favored **Campo San Felipe** (Av. Mar de Cortés 301, tel. 686/577-1012, www.camposanfelipe.com, US$15–20) has 34 full-hookup sites, and Internet access too. **Playa de Laura RV Park** (Av. Mar de Cortez 333, tel. 686/577-1128) offers just the basics, but it's still a popular place. Rates are about US$10 for tents, US$16–30 for RVs, depending on how close you are to the beach. At the far south end of town, **Club de Pesca RV and Trailer Park** (Av. Mar de Cortés, tel. 686/577-1180, fax 686/577-1888, clubdepescasf@yahoo.com, US$15–20) is removed from much of the action in San Felipe, but also close enough that you can walk to the shops and restaurants. It has 54 spots, many of them reserved for permanent residents. Call ahead.

FOOD
Seafood

Fish tacos, cold *cockteles,* and seafood platters anchor just about every San Felipe menu. **La Vaquita Restaurant & Bar** (Puerta Peñasco and Av. Mar de Cortés North, tel. 686/577-2837, Wed.–Mon. 11 A.M.–10 P.M.) serves breakfast, lunch, and dinner in an open-air setting. Seafood cocktails (US$6) are its specialty, but the menu also features fish plates (US$6–10) and tacos (US$4 per order). Close to the *malecón,* **(La Hacienda de la Langosta Roja** (Calz. Chetumal 121, tel. 686/577-0484, www.sanfelipelodging.com, daily 7 A.M.–11 P.M., dinner mains US$14–26) serves Italian-style seafood (piccata, Florentine, scampi, etc.) at reasonable prices. Its sunny patio is a plus on winter afternoons.

At **Chuy's Place** (Av. Mar de Cortés, no tel., daily for dinner, mains US$15) owner Jesus Davis does an amazing shrimp entr–e with oyster sauce and ginger, as well as lamb chops with mango sauce.

Mexican

On the *malecón,* **Rice and Beans** (tel. 686/577-1770, riceybeans@hotmail.com, Mon.–Fri. 7 A.M.–11 P.M., breakfast mains US$2–6, lunch/dinner mains US$14–16) serves breakfast, lunch, and dinner with tables inside (air-conditioned) and on a streetside terrace. Fresh fish and carne asada anchor a menu of Mexican fare.

Rockodile Patio and Grill (tel. 686/577-1219, www.4rockodile.com, daily noon–midnight, mains US$10–15), on the *malecón,* serves its fish tacos with a tray of condiments. Burgers with fries are another standby. Next to Bar Miramar on the north end of the *malecón,* **Rosita's Restaurant** (Av. Mar de Cortés 381, tel. 686/540-6218, www.rositarest.com, daily 9 A.M.–10 P.M., US$6–13) is a friendly, if touristy, place with decent Mexican food, including shrimp tacos.

Also on the *malecón,* two-story **Licoraria** (no tel.) is first and foremost a place to try fish tacos, but it also serves *machaca, chilaquiles,* and other types of tacos for US$1.50 apiece.

Rosita's Restaurant on the *malecón*

© PAUL ITOI

If you're on the hunt for an authentic Mexican meal, head to **La Fonda Los Portales** (Manzanillo, one block west of the toursit office, no tel., mains US$7–12), open daily for breakfast, lunch, and dinner. It's known for its rich chicken *mole* and other Mexican classics of Aztec origin. Traditional tortilla soup and refreshing *agua de jamaica* round out the menu. The restaurant does not serve alcoholic beverages, but you can bring your own.

International

At the golf course of La Ventana del Mar Resort, **Pavilion** (U.S. tel. 877/629-2852 or 619/299-5990, Mon.–Fri. 8 A.M.–7 P.M., Sat. 8 A.M.–9 P.M. Sun. 10 A.M.–9 P.M., mains US$10–18) offers a gourmet menu with entr–es such as fricassee of veal, walnut-encrusted rack of lamb, and champagne-poached scallops.

Perched high above the town, the **Lighthouse Lounge** (Guaymas 152, tel. 686/577-2540, lighthouselounge1@prodigy.net.mx, Tues.–Sun. 8 A.M.–10 P.M., mains US$10–15) has the most unique view around

and cheerful and festive decor. On the menu are omelettes, burgers, sandwiches, and salads, plus steaks and Mexican plates for dinner.

South of the Caribe Motel, **The George** (Av. Mar de Cortés, tel. 686/577-1057, daily 6 A.M.– 10 P.M., US$12–22) is a cross between a steakhouse and a diner, with leather booths and bright lighting. The menu includes Mexican fare, as well as steaks.

El Nido Steakhouse (Av. Mar de Cortés 348, tel. 686/577-1028, Thurs.–Tues. 2–10 P.M., mains US$18–25) is a Baja chain known for its Western decor and steaks grilled over a mesquite wood fire. Guests sit in tall leatherback chairs at heavy wood tables, under the dim light of red lamps.

Baja Mar/The Taco Factory specializes in shrimp dishes, and the guacamole is a standout. Tacos cost US$1–1.50 each. Entrees run US$8–20, and the seafood combo (US$48) is large enough for two. There is an enclosed dining room, but the larger dining area is outside on a large deck with a bar in the middle.

Try **Baja Burger** (Av. Mar de Cortés 162,

no tel., www.bajaburguer.com, daily for breakfast and lunch, mains US$3–9) for a quick bite, such as *chilaquiles* for breakfast or a burger with fries for lunch.

Cafés

Behind the Beachcomber Bar and on the second story of the building, **Baja Java** (Av. Mar de Cortés and Calz. Chetumal, no tel., baja_java@highes.net, daily for breakfast and lunch) is the place for espresso drinks. Enjoy the sea views from its sunny patio. Downstairs is the **Smoke Signals** (no tel.) cigar shop and lounge.

Groceries

Many of the stores you'll need for groceries and supplies are located along Calzada Chetumal on the way into town. At the entrance to town is **Ruben's Fish Market** (Mar Caribe Sur 158). Avenida Mar de Caribe also has several bakeries. Near the north end of the *malecón*, **La Vaquita Dos** (Puerto Peñasco 292, tel. 686/577-1710, daily until 11 P.M.) has meat and produce counters, as well as fresh tortillas made on-site. On the weekends, they'll barbecue your meat, free of charge. You can also pick up a variety of household supplies. Special orders are welcome.

INFORMATION AND SERVICES
Tourist Assistance

The Secretary of Tourism for San Felipe (Manzanillo 300 at Av. Mar de Cortés, tel. 686/577-1155 or -1865, turismosf@yahoo.com.mx, www.turismobc.gob.mx, Mon.–Fri. 8 A.M.–7 P.M., Sat. 9 A.M.–3 P.M., Sun. 10 A.M.–1 P.M.) distributes maps, brochures, and other visitor information.

Money

There are half a dozen ATMs around town, including a machine at the 7-Eleven/Pemex station as you enter town, a Bancomer on Avenida Mar de Cortés, and a Banamex on Calzada Chetumal. There is a *casa de cambio* on Calzada Chetumal, across from the Beachcomber.

Post and Telephone

You'll find San Felipe's post office (Mon.–Fri. 8 A.M.–1 P.M. and 2–6 P.M.) on Mar Blanco, one block south of Calzada Chetumal. For other mail and business services, try Yet Mail Etc. (Av. Mar de Cortés 75, tel. 686/577-1255).

Internet Access

Bandidos' Net (Av. Mar de Cortés, Plaza Canela 1, tel. 686/577-1600, www.sanfelipe.com.mx, Mon.–Fri. 8 A.M.–4 P.M., Sat. 9 A.M.–1 P.M., closed Sat. in summer), next to the El Cortez motel, charges US$4 per hour for high-speed wired or wireless access. At **Café Tazzo** (Av. Mar de Cortés and Calle Ensenada), next to the Caribe Moteo, you can use computer terminals or connect your own laptop via Wi-Fi while you enjoy coffee and dessert. It opens at 7 A.M. daily.

Emergencies

The **Abasolo Medical Clinic** (Calz. Chetumal, near the Pemex, tel. 686/577-1706, Mon.–Fri. 9 A.M.–2 P.M. and 4–8 P.M., emergencies any time) is run by the former head of the local hospital. He speaks excellent English and has been in the San Felipe area for two decades. He can also arrange for emergency ground or air transportation to San Diego if needed. **Hospital San Felipe** (tel. 686/577-0117 or -2849) and the **police station** (tel. 686/577-1134 or dial 060) are located next to each other on the south side of town. The Red Cross is on Puerto Peñasco.

GETTING THERE AND AROUND
By Air

San Felipe has an international airport (SFE, Mar Caribe Sur/Airport Road, tel. 686/577-1368 or -1568, danielpg60@hotmail.com, winter daily 7 A.M.–5 P.M., summer daily 8 A.M.–6 P.M.), but it isn't served by any commercial airlines. The closest major airport is Mexicali. **Grey Eagle Aviation** (U.S. tel. 760/804-8680 or 888/280-8802, www.greyeaglecharter.com) advertises an air taxi service from Long Beach or San Diego, California, to San Felipe on Tuesday, Friday, and Sunday. Services for private pilots include aviation gas and customs clearing. The trip to town is 9.2 kilometers, and costs US$15 by taxi.

By Bus

San Felipe has a bus depot on Avenida Mar Caribe Sur, south of Calzada Chetumal and near the Pemex. It's open daily 5 A.M.– 11 P.M. (when the last bus from Mexicali arrives, tel. 686/577-1516). **ABC** offers connections to Mexicali, Ensenada, and Tijuana. You can buy your ticket an hour before the bus departs. To reach the Tijuana office, call 664/683-5681. **Estrellas del Pacífico** (Tijuana tel. 664/683-5022 or -6789) also runs buses to San Felipe from Mexicali and Ensenada.

By Taxi

Taxis congregate on Calzada Chetumal near Los Mandiles, or you can call 686/577-1293 to order one. Local trips around town should cost under US$5.

SAN FELIPE TO PUERTECITOS

South of San Felipe, the coastal road deteriorates, though it is paved as far as Puertecitos (85 km south of San Felipe). Construction had commenced in early 2009 to pave the road beyond Puertecitos; however, only the first few kilometers were underway at press time, in the meantime, the old dirt road was in terrible shape. There is no gas until Punta Willard/ Alfonsina, so fill up your tank before leaving town, and bring some fuel to spare. Watch for *vados* (drainage dips) and potholes along the way. Accommodations are primitive camps, and supplies are few and far between.

Estero Percebú

About 16 kilometers south of San Felipe, a dirt road turn-off leads one kilometer east to a lagoon and white-sand beach with a small community of gringo homes. You can swim or kayak here, as long as you bring your own gear. The area is also known as Shell Island, which refers to a spit of land that's only accessible at low tide. Beachcombers will delight in the possibilities for collecting shells.

Rancho Percebú (Km 16, Carr. San Felipe-Puertecitos, tel. 686/577-1259, open year-round, US$10) has campsites, *palapas,* restrooms, and hot showers. There is also a restaurant/bar at the camp. The friendly Lopez family has run the ranch for several decades and counting. The campground is four kilometers east of the highway.

Valle de los Gigantes

Fifteen kilometers south of San Felipe, on the way to Puertecitos, photographers and naturalists will enjoy the chance to view the world's tallest cactus species up close. The *Pachycereus* or cardón grows to heights of more than 18 meters and can weigh up to 12 tons. Many live to be hundreds of years old.

Besides the namesake giants, the park holds ocotillo, palo verde, cholla, and many other cacti. Desert fauna includes mountain quail, eagles, owls, coyotes, road runners, and buzzards. Daytime temperatures will climb above 100°F in summer and to about 50°F in winter. Bring your own water for hiking the trails.

Look for a turnoff near Km 14 on the west side of the highway, and follow the unpaved road about 200 meters to the park entrance. The closest place to camp is Playa Punta Estrella (Km 13, Carr. San Felipe-Puertecitos, tel. 686/565-2784, US$10), with *palapas,* flush toilets, and hot showers, but no hookups. Soft sand could pose a problem for RVs here. The campground is 1.6 kilometers east of the highway.

For guided hikes in the Valle de los Gigantes, contact **Rupestres** (mobile tel. 044/686/158-9921, www.rupestres.com, explorandobajacalifornia@hotmail.com, US$60).

Camping

Continuing south, the coastline presents a series of beaches, most with primitive *campos* that charge US$5–10 a night, depending on the season and the facilities they offer. **Playa Destiny**

in the Valle de los Gigantes

(Km 71–72, Carr. San Felips-Puertecitos, no tel., US$15) has toilets, cold showers, grills, and picnic tables. **Playa Escondida** (Km 85–86, Carr. San Felipe-Puertecitos, no tel., US$10) occupies a white-sand cove. Outhouses and cold showers are about it for amenities, but there are fishing *pangas* for hire.

PUERTECITOS

Civilization, such as it is, appears again at Puertecitos, but don't get too excited. This fishing village has weather-worn homes and trailers, *panga* fishing boats, and natural hot springs (US$5) to offer weary travelers. The beach is small, and the only businesses are a restaurant (Oct.–Apr. daily 6 A.M.–10 P.M.) and a grocery store *(tienda de abarrotes)*.

Accommodations and Camping

The beach camp, **Campo Puertecitos** (Km 89, Carr. San Felipe-Puertecitos, tel. 686/577-1155 or -1865) has 14 sites for primitive camping (US$20), and four barebones rooms for rent. The property has *palapas* for shade and grills for cooking your fresh catch.

PUNTA BUFEO TO PUNTA FINAL

You need high clearance, sturdy tires, good shocks, and a lot of driving patience to continue south of Puertecitos. Plan on 5–6 hours of driving to make the 72.5-kilometer trip to Alfonsina's on Bahía Willard.

Punta Bufeo

Fishing fanatics enjoy the onshore catch off Punta Bufeo and around the **Islas Encantadas** just offshore. This group of islands provides the ideal habitat for yellowtail, croaker, corvina, and sierra.

The next settlement to the south, **Alfonsina's** (Tijuana tel. 664/648-1951) has supplies, including gas (but not diesel). Rancho Grande also may have gas if Alfonsina's is out.

ACCOMMODATIONS AND FOOD

Campo Punta Bufeo (56 km south of Puertecitos along the dirt road that parallels the coast) has campsites (US$5–10) on the beach, as well as a restaurant, toilets, showers, and simple motel rooms (US$20).

Punta Willard, the next point south, about 12 kilometers south of Punta Bufeo, has a legendary settlement called **Papa Fernández** (www.papafernandez.com). This campground on the beach has *palapa* shelters (US$5), outhouses (but no showers), a boat ramp, and *panga* fishing. The best part about Papa Fernández is its restaurant (daily dawn–dusk, and often later, mains US$6–14), which serves homemade tortillas and chile rellenos and will cook your catch.

Papa Fernández does not have its own telephone; however, in an emergency, you can dial the mini-mart at Rancho Grande on a satellite phone (tel. 555/151-4065). Leave a call-back number, as well as your name and the name of the person you are trying to contact. It's also a good idea to describe the vehicle that your contact is driving in Baja. On the message, ask

CEVICHE GONZAGA BAY STYLE

Ann Hazard's Baja cookbooks have become a peninsular favorite, with recipes collected from many famous restaurants and devised from the author's own travels and culinary adventures. Whether you want to prepare a few of your own meals on the road, or bring the flavors of Baja back to your own home, this basic ceviche recipe is a keeper. The acid from the lime juice "cooks" the fish, so there's no need for a heat source to prepare the meal.

INGREDIENTS

- 2 lbs cubed white fish or bay scallops, raw
- 2 cups juice from *limónes* (Mexican limes)
- 5-10 fresh serrano or jalapeño chiles, diced (remove seeds if you prefer it less spicy)
- 1 red bell pepper, diced
- 1 green bell pepper, diced
- 1 onion, diced
- 3 ripe tomatoes, diced
- 2 cloves garlic, minced
- 1 bunch cilantro, with stems removed, finely chopped
- 1 tsp brown sugar
- Salt and pepper to taste
- 2 avocados, diced
- Totopos (tortilla chips) or saltine crackers

INSTRUCTIONS

In a bowl, cover the cubed fish with lime juice. Cover and refrigerate for 2-3 hours, stirring occasionally. Fish should become quite white and scallops will lose their translucent appearance. (Once this happens, you will know the lime juice has "cooked" them and they are okay to eat.)

Transfer to a larger bowl and mix with all other ingredients except avocado. Immediately prior to serving, add diced avocados and remaining cilantro. Serve in a bowl surrounded with chips or saltine crackers.

– Reprinted with permission from *Cooking with Baja Magic Dos*, by Ann Hazard (www.bajamagic.com)

Rancho Grande to contact Papa Fernández on the marine radio.

Bahía San Luis Gonzaga

Popular with private pilots and experienced Baja adventurers, the flat, gray-sand beach along remote Bahía San Luis Gonzaga is reminiscent of an earlier time. A few dozen rustic beach homes line the shore—each with its private plane, boat, or dune buggy parked outside. **Rancho Grande** (tel. 555/151-4065) offers beach camping for US$5 a night. Facilities include outhouses, showers, and a mini-market.

Punta Final is a small cape with several points and a small lagoon. It marks the south end of Gonzaga Bay and offers good views of the bay from above.

TO MEXICO 1

From Bahía San Luis Gonzaga, it's 64.5 kilometers (approximately 90 min) of graded dirt-road driving to the Transpeninsular Highway. The road intersects Mexico 1 at Km 229–230 in the town of Chapala.

About halfway from the coast to the highway, you'll come across **Coco's Corner,** a café that's famous for its beer can decor (and desert plants too). Stop here for cold beer, soda, and burritos. Camping costs US$5 a night if you've run out of daylight. Owner Coco moved to the desert from Ensenada in 1990, following an accident in which he lost one leg. He speaks some English and knows the area extremely well. When you sign his guestbook, he will draw a picture of your vehicle next to the entry.

www.moon.com

DESTINATIONS | ACTIVITIES | BLOGS | MAPS | BOOKS

MOON.COM is all new, and ready to help plan your next trip! Filled with fresh trip ideas and strategies, author interviews, informative blogs, a detailed map library, and descriptions of all the Moon guidebooks, Moon.com is all you need to get out and explore the world—or even places in your own backyard. As always, when you travel with Moon, expect an experience that is uncommon and truly unique.

MAP SYMBOLS

▨ Expressway	◖ Highlight	✗ Airfield	⚓ Golf Course
⋯ Primary Road	○ City/Town	✈ Airport	℗ Parking Area
═ Secondary Road	◉ State Capital	▲ Mountain	▰ Archaeological Site
⋯ Unpaved Road	✹ National Capital	✛ Unique Natural Feature	⛪ Church
------- Trail	★ Point of Interest		
⋯⋯ Ferry	• Accommodation	⇗ Waterfall	⛽ Gas Station
⊏⊐ Railroad	▼ Restaurant/Bar	▲ Park	◌ Glacier
▨ Pedestrian Walkway	■ Other Location	☐ Trailhead	⬢ Mangrove
⊞ Stairs	Λ Campground	⛷ Skiing Area	▨ Reef
			▭ Swamp

CONVERSION TABLES

°C = (°F - 32) / 1.8
°F = (°C x 1.8) + 32
1 inch = 2.54 centimeters (cm)
1 foot = 0.304 meters (m)
1 yard = 0.914 meters
1 mile = 1.6093 kilometers (km)
1 km = 0.6214 miles
1 fathom = 1.8288 m
1 chain = 20.1168 m
1 furlong = 201.168 m
1 acre = 0.4047 hectares
1 sq km = 100 hectares
1 sq mile = 2.59 square km
1 ounce = 28.35 grams
1 pound = 0.4536 kilograms
1 short ton = 0.90718 metric ton
1 short ton = 2,000 pounds
1 long ton = 1.016 metric tons
1 long ton = 2,240 pounds
1 metric ton = 1,000 kilograms
1 quart = 0.94635 liters
1 US gallon = 3.7854 liters
1 Imperial gallon = 4.5459 liters
1 nautical mile = 1.852 km

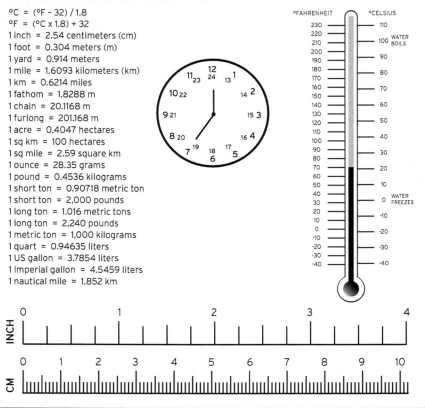

MOON ENSENADA & NORTHERN BAJA
Avalon Travel
a member of the Perseus Books Group
1700 Fourth Street
Berkeley, CA 94710, USA
www.moon.com

Editor: Erin Raber
Series Manager: Kathryn Ettinger
Copy Editor: Ellie Behrstock
Graphics and Production Coordinator:
   Domini Dragoone
Cover Designer: Domini Dragoone
Map Editor: Albert Angulo
Cartographer: Kat Bennett

ISBN: 978-1-59880-326-6

Some photos and illustrations are used by permission and are the property of the original copyright owners.

Front cover photo: © James Steidel/BigStockPhoto. com.
Title page photo: © 123rf.com/Connie Wade, Ensenada Coastline.

Printed in the United States

KEEPING CURRENT

If you have a favorite gem you'd like to see included in the next edition, or see anything that needs updating, clarification, or correction, please drop us a line. Send your comments via email to feedback@moon.com, or use the address above.

ABOUT THE AUTHOR

Nikki Goth Itoi

The living coral reef at Cabo Pulmo drew Nikki Goth Itoi and her husband, Paul, to Baja for the first time in 2000. In 2002, they both quit business jobs to drive Mexico's Baja and mainland coasts for several months. Seven thousand miles and countless tacos later, they remembered the people, cuisine, and tropical-desert scenery of Baja best of all – and they have returned as often as possible ever since.

Nikki Goth Itoi has experience writing for print, radio, and online media. Her work has been published in the *San Francisco Chronicle*, *Red Herring*, *IndustryWeek*, *Business 2.0*, *Hemispheres*, and other publications. She is the author of *Moon Hudson River Valley* and a contributing editor to *Gemütlichkeit: The Travel Letter for Germany, Austria, Switzerland, and the New Europe*. A native of New York State, Nikki has traveled throughout Mexico, Europe, Asia, and the United States for work and fun.

When not on the road, Nikki enjoys outdoor activities, including swimming, bike rides, and backcountry skiing. She and Paul live in Davis, CA with their son, Emmett.